TAROT READING MADE EASY

IT'S ALL IN THE CARDS

JOHN MANGIAPANE

IT'S ALL IN THE
CARDS

Tarot Reading Made Easy

JOHN MANGIAPANE

STERLING PUBLISHING CO., INC.
NEW YORK

I dedicate this book to my students—past, present, and future. It is said: "If you become a teacher, by your pupils you shall be taught." Thank you for everything you have shared with me on my "Fool's Journey."

In various places in this book, cards are discussed that may indicate mental or physical illness or other conditions, such as pregnancy, or even abuse. This is for your information alone. You are *not* a physician and are not qualified to make a medical diagnosis or dispense medical advice. DO NOT CROSS THIS LINE! In the course of your readings, you will get many Querents who will disallow the expert medical advice available to them and request that you tell them "what is wrong" with them. In their minds you have some occult connection. They are falling into the centuries-old practice of searching for a soothsayer, and you are opening yourself up to a lawsuit. Where is that fine line? As soon as you tell people they are pregnant, mentally unstable, should spend a sum of money, or give recommendations on how to influence or beat the system, you have crossed that line.

Illustrations from the Rider-Waite Tarot Deck ®, known also as the Rider Tarot and the Waite Tarot, reproduced by permission of U. S. Games Systems, Inc., Stamford, CT 06902 USA. Copyright © 1971 by U. S. Games Systems, Inc. Further reproduction prohibited. The Rider-Waite Tarot Deck is a registered trademark of U.S. Games Systems, Inc.

Library of Congress Cataloging-in-Publication Data

Mangiapane, John.
  It's all in the cards: tarot : reading made easy / John Mangiapane.
    p. cm.
  Includes index.
  ISBN 1-4027-0986-2
  1. Tarot. I. title.
BF1879.T2 M332 2004
133.3'242—dc22

                                                        2003024881

10 9 8 7 6 5 4 3 2

Published by Sterling Publishing Co., Inc.
387 Park Avenue South, New York, NY 10016
© 2004 by John Mangiapane
Distributed in Canada by Sterling Publishing
C/o Canadian Manda Group, 165 Dufferin Street,
Toronto, Ontario, Canada M6K 3H6
Distributed in Great Britain by Chrysalis Books Group PLC
The Chrysalis Building, Bramley Road, London W10 6SP, England
Distributed in Australia by Capricorn Link (Australia) Pty. Ltd.
P.O. Box 704, Windsor, NSW 2756, Australia

Manufactured in the United States of America
All rights reserved

Sterling ISBN 1-4027-0986-2

CONTENTS

FOREWORD

I love Tarot; I once purchased a large button at a psychic fair that read, "I like to read books, but I *love* to read Tarot cards!" My introduction into Tarot was backwards; I was using Tarot cards for other purposes before I started to learn to "read" them. I had bought *Tarot Spells* by Janina Rene, which featured a then-as-yet-unpublished deck designed by Robin Wood. It was a beautiful deck, to be sure, but I was interested in spell work and not divination at that time.

Eventually, I would hear the call of the cards, but the idea of studying such a large and esoteric subject interested and confused me at the same time. I started to buy other decks to check them out. I found that each deck came packaged with its own "little white booklet" of explanations for card interpretation. Some of the information was very sketchy and poor indeed; was I supposed to *learn* something from these little booklets? Many of them listed 10 or 12 single-word explanations, but none of them helped me to see the whole. To try to learn them this way was very discouraging.

I started to buy books on Tarot and ran into similar problems—lots of words, but little understanding. I found out the best way to learn Tarot was to go out and do it. I started keeping journals of what the readings said. I did this strictly for myself, since I could not pry myself away from the little white booklet for fear I would say something "wrong."

One day I was a merchant at a small psychic fair (and not making a cent), but I saw that the readers were busy with people signed up hours ahead of time. A woman hung out at my booth and told me how "disappointed" she was in whatever reading she had just been given; it didn't "work for her," she said. I suggested she try something that might answer her question more directly, like Tarot. She disappeared for about an hour and came back and told me that the next psychic "didn't tell her anything she didn't already know," as though she was expecting something "mystical" to happen. She asked about the Tarot deck I had for sale and could *I* do a reading for her—which, of course, I refused to do. First of all, I didn't like the deck, which is why I was selling it; and second, I did not feel I had enough experience to do a public reading. As the fair ended and I started to pack my unsold merchandise, she appeared again. I decided to give it a try. I took the deck I didn't like and we went out to the lobby of the hotel, and I did a reading for her. On the first card I said that her situation was work related; she said it wasn't. I continued through the reading and discovered she was having an affair with a coworker (the *first* card—right?). The cards indicated it was foolish and would end in disaster. She paid me and left. Suddenly, I was a reader! (And—I did not use the little white booklet!)

I did a lot of work after that: read a lot of books, did a lot of readings, and did a lot of studying. It was a long time before I ventured out to read for the public again. Eventually, I would feel more comfortable. (Someone once said to me, "Oh! You don't use the book?" "Why bother?" was my reply.) I had started to develop my own theories and understanding of what I was reading. One day it dawned on me that the one sure way to know if I understood what I was doing was to try to teach it to someone who had no background in Tarot. I formulated a class syllabus, presented it to a local adult education program, and waited for a response from the board of education. It was a while coming, but I was granted permission to teach an eight-week course in basic Tarot card reading. Creating the class was an experience in itself! In the years that followed, I modified, clarified, rewrote, discarded, and added new material as I went along.

This book is a distillation of that process.

THE TAROT DECK

THE origins of Tarot and the cards in the present decks are vague and uncertain. Many complicated and bizarre theories exist as to when and why they were created and how they came to this country or to that civilization. There are many books on the subject and I will not go into it here.

The "modern" decks (the ones we are most familiar with) consist of 78 cards. There are two distinct parts to the deck: The Major Arcana (*arcane*—Latin for "secrets") and the Minor Arcana. There are 22 cards in the Major Arcana (numbered 0 to 21), which bear names such as "The Magician" and "The Tower." There are 56 cards in the Minor Arcana that fall into four suits—which often get compared to a deck of modern playing cards. The four suits consist of pip cards numbered 1 to 10, plus four Court cards, usually a Page, Knight, Queen, and King, although some decks have Princes and Princesses.

There are literally hundreds upon hundreds of decks out there, and new ones come out every day. Many have beautiful artwork and little substance; some are minimalist at best; some are masterfully wrought. Most beginners start with the Rider-Waite deck, since it is the easiest to find in most large chain and small new age bookstores. Most of the symbolism I explain here is from this deck or one of its clones; however, feel free to use whatever deck suits your fancy or pocketbook.

In the Minor Arcana things run in fours. As I mentioned above, there are four suits that correspond to regular decks of playing cards (although that gets disputed, too): Cups, Swords, Pentacles (or Coins), and Wands. There are also four keys or essences, four elements, and four seasons that have their ties to a certain suit. *Regardless* of the question, no matter how complex or intricate, there are only *four* simple situations that everyone wants answers about: Money, Work, Love Relationships, and the Future!

These areas are given special consideration in this book.

I've been asked whether the Querent* (the questioner) doesn't ask questions about health or the health of loved ones. Some Tarot cards do touch on health issues, but since it is unwise and illegal for Tarot readers to diagnose health conditions, I decided not to create a category for health.

A chart of correspondences could look something like this:

TAROT	SUIT	KEY	QUESTIONS	ELEMENT	SEASON
Cups	Hearts	Emotions	Love	Water	Summer
Swords	Spades	Action	Strategy	Fire	Winter
Pentacles	Diamonds	Manifestation	Money	Earth	Spring
Wands	Clubs	Ideas	Work	Air	Autumn

Studying the Cards

It would be unusual for anyone interested in Tarot to sit and try to learn the meanings for all the cards before attempting to do a reading. Most people skip to the sections on spreads and then flip back and forth trying to make sense of the cards and get some idea of what they think the cards are telling them. At least 90 percent of us started this way; the truly psychic are few and far between. You learn Tarot by studying and doing.

I tell my students to keep a journal—along with, but separate from, their class notes—and write everything in it that comes to mind while they work with the cards, including the weather, the phase of the Moon, and so on. If you write it down, you don't forget it. Many times students tell me they did a fantastic reading during the week for a family member, but they failed to record it for the class to study. A journal keeps you abreast of your progress. Perhaps a reading you did in the past will appear more defined as you read about it at some future time, or you will see that you were more accurate then you imagined.

The best place to begin is with meditation. You can start with the Fool and work your way through the entire deck or you can

*The Querent is the person you are reading for. Some say the word is an obsolete legal term for "a plaintiff," or does not exist at all. In the Tarot world, the Querent is defined as "the one who inquires" or "queries."

shuffle the cards each day and meditate on a random card. Prop the card up against something, or find a placecard holder or some other holder to keep it upright; one student placed hers in a Lucite frame so that she could see it every time she walked past. Begin by studying the image—what does it say to you? What is your immediate impression of the central character on the card? What was the first thing you thought of? Some people go deep into the card— that is, they imagine walking into the card like Alice through the looking glass, observing the environment, and asking the character in the illustration about the card. Regardless of what method you use or are most comfortable with, the important thing is to *write it down*—or speak your meditation into a tape recorder and write it down later. Intuition is what you are trying to develop. Do not be surprised if you find your impressions are the opposite of what books (even mine) may tell you; in fact, write down both meanings so you can compare them. The point is that you don't want to limit yourself to any one person's interpretation. Soon you will have a notebook full of entries to which you can refer.

It's also a good idea to record the readings you do, particularly readings for yourself—what cards are in which position and how you felt or what you thought, and also what the Querent (the person you're reading for) said about your analysis. Perhaps you will start to see trends or a repeated card in many readings, each with a different interpretation.

Perhaps as you move into deeper Tarot study, you will come to own more than one deck, and many of the decks will have different images than those you are used to: meditate on them, too. Put two of the same cards side by side and record what you see as similarities and what you see as differences, and why you feel this way. The great experiment is to do a reading with one deck, and then pull the same cards from another deck and see if you interpret the reading any differently. Sometimes no matter how often a card has come up, little things will start jumping out at you, such as the fact that the card has red banners, or that the gold sash gleams more today than you ever noticed it did before. All of these things are clues for you to interpret.

An extension of the one-card-a-day ritual is to shuffle the cards and ask: "What lesson will I need to learn today?" Then record the card. At the end of the day (or whenever you journal your day), see how it worked out. I have been doing this for years. Sometimes the cards are dead-on; sometimes they falter. The point is that the more you work with the cards the better your readings will be. No matter how gifted or psychic you are, you cannot become a reader overnight. The best part is that you can interpret Tarot for the rest of your life and learn something new every day. That is one of the great attractions of Tarot. My mother once asked me: "Do you run your life by this stuff?" and, of course, the answer is "no." But forewarned is forearmed. Perhaps today you will pull a card that hints that work might not run so smoothly. Your day may or may not go by without a glitch in it. If something unpleasant does comes up, you will have been warned to "expect" it, so it may not bother you as much because you have been mentally preparing for it. If your day goes by smoothly, perhaps the appearance of that card prepared you to accept minor inconveniences without complaint.

Shuffling

Before we get into anything else, let us talk about the most basic aspect of Tarot cards—shuffling. Everyone knows how to shuffle—right? Wrong!

People who are used to shuffling standard playing cards each have their own variation—some lay them out flat on the table and move them around like in "Concentration." Some do the "casino shuffle," where they split the pack in half and riffle the long edges or two corners together and mix the cards. Some flex the two halves and snap them together. All of these techniques *do* shuffle the cards together.

The most-heard comment from Querents when you ask them to shuffle is "Wow! These cards are *big*!" Tell them to shuffle in whatever way is most comfortable to them.

Used to standard playing cards that have no upright or reversed position, people unwittingly flip part of the deck around—and this is where reversals come from. Some readers lay out the cards and then flip the reversals so that the cards are all upright. I get no reversed cards with my particular shuffling technique, but since Querents do, it is best to understand reversed meanings. This is how to prevent reversals:

Go through your whole deck and make sure the cards are all upright. Place the deck in front of you so that the tops of the cards are away from you. Pick up the deck with your left hand so that the tops are at your index finger and the bottoms are at your thumb. Lay the deck on its left long edge.

With your right hand take approximately half the deck and

separate it by sliding the cards along the table—similar to closing a sliding door; the tops of this half of the deck will be at your right thumb and the bottoms at your right index finger. Do not spin this half of the deck around! Flex the deck, and riffle the "thumb" ends together. Push the two halves together. Congratulations! You now have shuffled the deck without turning half the deck over to be reversed! Do this as many times as feels comfortable. No matter how many times you do it, the tops are at your left index finger and the bottoms will be at your left thumb. When you are through, place the deck in front of you.

This is where the next mistake is usually made—card orientation. Do you flip the cards over side to side as though you are turning pages in a book, or do you flip them over top to bottom? When you shuffle my way, *always* turn over the cards side to side to preserve their upright positions. If you flip them over end to end, you will reverse all the cards. In fact, try this both ways right now and see what happens.

Think about this: if the Querent hands you back the deck and you flip the cards end to end, you are reversing all the cards *including* the reversed ones: is this what you want to do? Reason says do whatever you have been doing all along, since it is what works for you. That may be true if you are reading for yourself—the cards will give you the answer you need. However, since the shuffling of Querents can vary widely, you may be better off telling them, "hand me the cards with what you consider the top to be facing me." This way you will have the deck in correct orientation. (Some readers will tell you to turn the entire deck around if the first card comes up reversed, and give it an upright position. Some readers refuse to read a reversed first card.) You may or may not cut the deck; it is a personal preference. If you do, tradition suggests you cut the deck with your left hand to the left; the number of piles is irrelevant. You or the Querent can take the piles to reassemble the deck.

Now you are ready to do a spread and conduct a reading!

USING TAROT SPREADS

WHY do we use Tarot spreads (or layouts)? The purpose is to find a focus to effectively answer the question—*not* to get the answer we want to receive. This is what many Querents are looking for, or expect that a reading is going to do for them.

My roommate's sister uses no spread at all; she "throws" the cards and does a "stream of consciousness" thing, laying out 6–8 cards in a row and talking and talking and laying another row on top of them until she has gone through the entire 78 cards. Effective if it works for you, but definitely not for beginners! The readers you see in television commercials do this (at least on camera)—they don't sit there painstakingly analyzing each and every card. Instead, they use the cards as a springboard and say what first pops into their minds.

Most of us start with a simple approach. What is simpler than a single card?

One-Card Spreads

A one-card spread will give you an immediate answer with no frills or fancy explanations, as in the preceding example of "What lesson will I need to learn today?"

Yes/No Questions

It's not a good idea to use the Tarot to answer yes/no questions (flip a coin instead), but if you choose to, take only the Major Arcana, shuffle them, and then flip them over one by one until you come to the Fool (No) or the World (Yes).

Two-Card Spreads

Although a one-card spread may be great for people on the go, when an immediate answer is sought, it is limiting. A two-card layout (also known as a Cover & Cross spread) can give you more information. (It is also the basis for the Celtic Cross that we will get to soon.)

Shuffle and ask your question.

Turn up the first card and place it upright: this is the answer and/or describes the current situation.

Place the second card *sideways* over the first card; this is a challenge or an obstacle you will encounter. Read these two cards together as a unit. (**Note:** The second card is *neither* upright nor reversed; it is interpreted as an *influence* on the first card.)

Three-Card Spreads

The usual three-card spread is interpreted as Past—Present—Future and gives most people what they are looking for; it is also good when you don't have much experience reading the cards, since information pared down to one card at a time is easy to interpret.

The next step up is the three-card Cover & Cross spread that follows the development of a situation. Shuffle and ask the question; lay the first three cards upright left to right #1, #2, #3, as shown below. Lay #4 across #1, card #5 across #2, and card #6 across #3. Interpret this spread as:

#1 the past
#4 as the recent past
#2 as the present
#5 as the challenge you are facing
#3 as what you will do
#6 as the result or outcome

Surprise! Almost all spreads are variations on some version of these!

Creating Your Own Spreads

There is nothing to stop you from creating your own spreads. Start with a purpose: what kind of question do you have and how many cards do you feel it will it take to give you the answer? Let us say you want to know how things are going, but you also want to know how the past, present, and future are influencing each other. The present and the outcome make two cards, so what else would you like to know? Influences coming in and leaving the picture? How about unknown influences? That makes five cards.

Next, you could lay them out in a straight line, but that's boring! Life is circular, so maybe a circle is the best layout. You could come up with something like this:

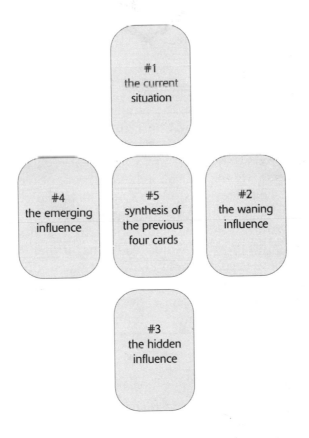

In *Power Tarot* by MacGregor and Vega, this is called the Wheel Spread, and my classes found it very useful because it gave them sufficient information without overpowering them. Interpreting the final card as a synthesis of the previous four can be tricky, but we all found it very accurate.

But why or how does creating a new spread *work*? It will work because you have made the decision about how many cards to use, and what each one will tell you in its placement; you are going into the shuffling with this thought in mind. The answers you seek will fall into place; this is why it's a good idea to record such observations in a journal. You may become so adept at using your own spreads that you might never use any of the other hundreds of recognized spreads out there. No one universal spread is appropriate for all occasions. Most readers learn to use what is called the Celtic Cross—a 10-card spread, which is probably the most popular.

The Celtic Cross Spread

Here is the great-grandmother of all Tarot spreads and the one even non-Tarot people may be familiar with through movies and television. It has seen many transformations; some variations have 9 to 12 cards, but we are going to stick with the basic 10.

First, there is the question of a Significator card. This is a card chosen to personify the individual being read for by matching physical or other characteristics of the Querent to the character in the card illustration. I seldom use a Significator card. I feel that to remove a card from the deck could be detrimental to the reading. Since the Significator card is not read, what if that card represents something the Querent should know, and you're now removing it? The one time I believe the Significator card is useful is when you are doing a reading in absentia (with the Querent's permission). More about the Significator is found in the section on Court Cards, page 137.

In the Celtic Cross Spread, the Significator is placed in the center of the table, and card #1 is placed over it; this is why many books call the first card the "Cover" card, since it is what covers you. (That is why the two-card reading is called "Cover & Cross.") The second card is placed sideways over the first (what "crosses" you). In the traditional layout, cards 3, 4, 5, and 6 are usually laid out so that the spread looks like this:

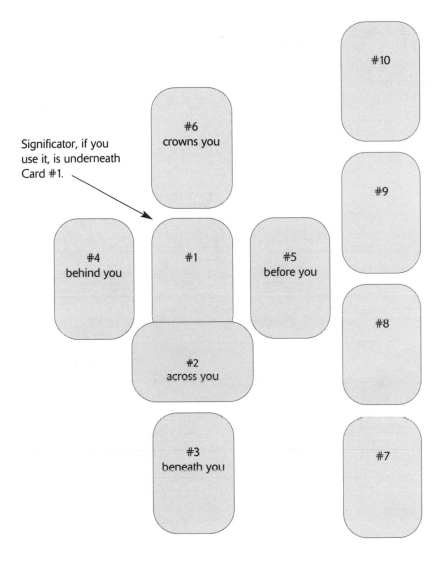

Significator, if you use it, is underneath Card #1.

#6 crowns you

#4 behind you

#1

#5 before you

#2 across you

#3 beneath you

#10

#9

#8

#7

Card #3 is what is beneath you, or the basis of the question—in other words, the entire past.

Card #4 is what is behind you—the recent past.

Card #5 is what is before you—either the present or the very near future.

Card #6 is above the Significator and is what "crowns" you— the future. Cards 7–10 are placed to one side of the reading with #7 at the base and #10 at the top. These are sometimes called the Scepter or the Wand.

I have my own variation of the Celtic Cross based on the readings I do for the public. I find that most readers sit opposite the Querent, so the Querent sees the reading upside down. I seat the Querent next to me. The placement of cards #3–6 tends to confuse the Querent, so I simplify it and run the Scepter up the side closest to the Querent:

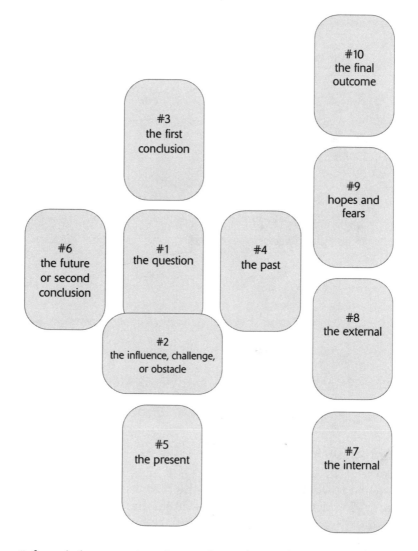

I found that running the cards in this style made it simpler for the Querent to understand what I was reading and saying. Before I explain my interpretation, I want to make a point: *where* you place the cards is important—but the order in which you lay them out and read them is *very* important. Once, I witnessed someone doing a Celtic Cross reading who laid out the cards in the traditional arrangement and then started reading them in a different order! I said that if you believe card #4 is the past, the fourth card you turn over is card #4 and should be interpreted as #4. We argued this for a while. It was her way of doing her readings, so it was best for her to do them that way. I feel that the fourth card off the deck is #4, so no matter *where* you place it, it is still card #4: please be consistent!

My Celtic Cross variation:

Card #1 is the *question* or what the question is all about. I never ask Querents their question ahead of time; I feel that would influence my interpretation of the answer. I say to them, "The first card deals with _____." At the conclusion of the reading, I ask them if the reading had anything to do with their question. I have found that 90 percent of the time this card reveals what they were asking about, even though they may deny it at first.

Card #2—the crossed card. Here we find an influence, challenge, or obstacle, and it might be positive or negative; after all, this card is *sideways*, neither upright nor reversed. It has a direct effect on card #1, and the combination of these two cards leads us directly to card #3.

Card #3—the first conclusion card. I feel that the Celtic Cross has three distinct conclusions: sometimes all point in the same direction, and sometimes they seem to be in disharmony with each other. This first conclusion is about to happen or is currently happening.

Card #4—the past card. Time in Tarot is relative. The past is anything that leads up to the previous moment, not necessarily something that goes back to early childhood. The past could be everything up to the time the Querent came in for a reading!

Card #5—the present card. The present could be both here and now or in the immediate future, since time moves forward. This card tells you what is going on in the Querent's life in regard to the question.

Card #6—the future or second conclusion card. The first conclusion card dealt with the outcome or the future on a short-term basis. Now that you know the past and present, this second conclusion card reveals the next step—how these events impact each other and what result can be expected. Querents may not like what is being revealed! It is important to remember that the cards are showing the future if events are not altered in some way and the situation is allowed to proceed unaided or unhindered. If, for example, you find that Querents are being deceived at work, you need to suggest that they take a closer look at those around them—not to make them paranoid, but for them to be aware that the cards are giving them a warning. Should they eventually find out the cards are revealing the truth, they can work to correct the situation; once they do, they have effectively altered the outcome. Carl Jung wrote that Tarot is of the moment; it reveals what is and what will happen if the situation remains unchanged.

As for the final four cards: here, as in everything else, no two readers agree! I have always felt that Cards 7 and 8 need to be read in tandem with each other since they reveal two sides of the same coin.

Card #7—the Internal, or how the Querent perceives the situation—not hopes and fears (that's card #9), but rather how the situation is impacting him or her. To understand this further, let's go to card #8 and read them together.

Card #8—the External, or how others around the Querent see the situation. These two cards can be shockingly opposed. The Querent may be in a bad marriage and feel unloved (internal), but the face shown to the world (external) may be one of happiness and loving kindness. This could be deliberate on the part of the Querent, who might be consciously covering up the true situation. Also, card #8 reveals only what the world sees, and it could very well be getting it wrong. Many interesting revelations come from these two cards together. What you say and do—and how it gets interpreted—are two different things.

In one reading, the Five of Swords and the Nine of Cups came up and I told the Querent she was living a lie. She then told me that when she and her husband went to parties, he made her the butt of his jokes, deliberately humiliating her in public, and she hated him for it. I have sometimes wondered which one the man with the swords represented—the husband with his cutting remarks, or the wife, with her desire to cut his tongue out!

Card #9—the Hopes and Fears card. Regardless of how the Querent feels (card #7), this card describes the Querent's projection of the final outcome, realistic or not. Generally, a positive card is a Hope and a negative card is a Fear; however, the important thing to remember is that this card is usually an illusion. Perhaps all the cards so far have been supportive or positive and this one is a "clinker." For example, the card reveals he is afraid the mortgage request will not be approved, or she thinks all her problems will be solved once and for all by a knight on a white horse who will gallop in and rescue her. The Hopes and Fears card is transitory at best. It is the stepping stone to the Final Outcome.

Card #10—the Final Outcome card. Herein lies the answer, if nothing is done to alter the events that lead to it. Regardless of the two prior conclusions, this one gives you the answer to the question, the final outcome.

What if conclusions #3 and #6 were great and #10 comes up The Tower card? How do you handle the situation? What if *all* the cards in the reading are clear sailing and the final card blows them out of the water? It can happen.

At this point I usually ask the Querent if the reading had anything to do with the question. If it didn't, or only partially touched on it, I ask what the question was and reinterpret the cards from that standpoint, asking them for input. Regardless of the spin you put on the cards, the lousy final outcome may still be waiting—you may not be able to sidestep it. If this happens (and it has), I truthfully tell the Querent that while the situation in the present *seems* to be what they want, perhaps they are overlooking something, and in the long run it may not produce the results they expect. To get such a drastic "slam" is a wake-up call to review the situation carefully.

What if you get a Court card (King, Queen, Knight, or Page) in the final position? Many readers (myself included) feel that if a Court card pops up as the last card, it is not the outcome, but a person who will influence or *bring about* the outcome. I recommend that you do another reading, using the Court card as the Significator. Gather and reshuffle the remaining cards, and ask them to show how this person is part of the answer. See if you get the outcome this time.

Asking the Question

You just grab your deck, think of a question, shuffle, lay out the cards, and read your answer, don't you? It looks that way, but it is not quite that simple. The way you ask the question and its wording are very important in getting a clear answer. Much of it will depend on the situation that brings a Querent to a reading, and the environment in which the reading is being done.

When people make contact for a reading, they probably have a question in mind; this is true of most one-on-one readings. However, I do readings at psychic fairs, parties in private homes, and I even participated in a local Mardi Gras a few times. In a group situation many of the people I read for give me a quizzical look when I ask them for a question and say, "I can't think of one!" This is not a good basis for starting a reading. Then again, some people are surprised that they have to touch the cards at all—don't you as the reader have all the answers? And some people simply blank out. A one-on-one reading is a serious matter; a "cattle-call" generally results in less important matters. I usually guide the clueless into a general question that has a time limit, such as, "Tell me about my life for the next twelve months," or "Give me an overview of my job for the next fiscal quarter." People in a group may be interested in some information, but are mostly looking to be entertained.

But what about when you're reading for yourself? What type of questions can you ask? Although the sky is the limit, I find that Tarot has certain limitations and does not deal well with any of the following:

Yes/No questions—As I said earlier, if you can answer the question with only a yes or no, flip a coin instead. Tarot deals with the past, present, and future, and Yes/No doesn't work based on this information. If you find you tend to ask this type of question: Should I quit this job? Y/N, think about wording it differently. For example: Will my job conditions improve or modify in the coming two months? This will allow the Tarot to speak about past, present, and future conditions.

Frivolous questions—Most people don't know if they believe you or not: if you have some psychic connection, or are merely making things up. In a party situation you will always find someone who will be skeptical, obnoxious, rude, or try to play you for a fool. Do not dishonor the cards by wasting their time or knowledge on such people. Be serious, be professional—give them a quick three-card reading and get them away from you. When you start getting asked questions such as, "Should I dye my hair purple?"—pack up your cards and take a break.

Open-ended questions—Beware the open-ended question! Be specific! Ask a question with a specific time frame: "Will we have enough money in two years to be able to move from this house?" not "Will I ever have a million dollars?" The future is not written in stone (you'll hear a reader say this many times); you affect your future constantly. No one can give you an accurate prediction for about 20 years or more from now—there are too many variables in such a long time span.

Run-on questions—This is a variation on the open-ended question: "Will I meet the person of my dreams and get married and live in a house with 2 dogs and 2.3 kids with a white picket fence and what will their names be?" What is the real question here? (Incidentally, the question "Am I going to die?" is an open-ended question, but the answer is "Yes. We all die sometime.")

Tarot deals best with questions concerning situations, challenges, improvements, and of course, outcomes. These are questions that ask who, what, where, when, why, how, and also will I, can I, and am I.

Who can help me with my financial problems?
What would be the benefit of _____?
Where will I be in _____ months?
When will my ship come in?
Why am I dreaming about ocean travel?
How does _____ feel about us/me?

Will it help me to apply for a job with a rival company?
Will I be able to do this job effectively?
Can I afford to buy such a large house?
Am I going to be successful with this business?

With some questions, there are two options and two outcomes. People who are unsure of which way to proceed usually ask these.

The Horseshoe Layout can help in such situations. A typical question is: "Should I stay with my present employer *or* should I look for a new job?" Here, the Querent wants to find out about the future with the present employer, and also whether changing jobs will be a good choice or a mistake. Shuffle, ask the question, and then lay out six cards in this order:

The Horseshoe Layout

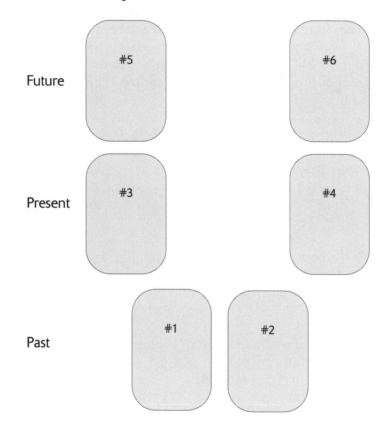

Although you lay the cards out #1–6, you read up each arm separately, #1, 3, and 5 being the first side of the question (staying with current employer in the above question), and #2, 4, and 6 being the alternative (what can be expected if the new job is taken). Of course, in this question I doubt if the new employment can really have a "past," but Card #2 probably could be read as the "past" the Querent brings along to the new job.

I used this layout for a friend who had been phone-solicited by a headhunter for a job that seemed too good to be true. Three people he talked with told him that he was a shoo-in for the job. He wished to know if the job was really on the up-and-up, if the money was real or merely an enticement. His reading:

We read the left side as his current job—the right side as the new job. Clearly, card #5 shows him leaving his job, and card #6 shows good news brought by the clarifier card*, which, in this case, was the Wheel of Fortune.

*Clarifier cards—Anytime you come up against a card that you feel needs more information to be better understood, flip the top card off the pack on top of that particular card and see what comes up. I often do this with Pages and Knights. Just be sure to lay out all the cards necessary for the reading first, then turn over a clarifier from the unused cards if you need one. Do not turn over the next card before you have completed the initial layout.

Well, we were half-right! My friend did leave his job and take the offer; it *was* everything he wished for, but unfortunately the company was horrible to work for and his coworkers were even worse. Within two weeks he got *another* job offer and quit on the spot! (Card #5?)

Whatever you do, never ask an emotionally charged question if you don't want to hear the truth. Also, do not read if you are angry, upset, or feeling out of sorts; not only will your emotional state affect the cards (particularly if you are reading for yourself), but your ability to interpret them clearly will be compromised.

You will notice when you shuffle cards that some come up in reverse; there are different meanings when this happens. I give them here and to my classes for reference. As I mentioned before, I do not read reversed cards, since I never get them when I shuffle, but when I do readings for others they invariably do occur, so it's good to know what they mean.

Remember when I said that all questions boil down to four subjects? I give you these to help you understand the card. A student once asked me if this was the way to learn them; that is, if it's a love question, it means "this," and if it's a work question, it means "that." The answer is "yes—and no." For example, the Fool card is a card about fresh starts, so how do you put a spin on this singular concept to make it apply more universally? You'll learn how to do it as you go along—we are all "spin doctors." A card's meaning changes with its position in a layout; it changes every time, even if it appears in the next five readings you do. Does it mean the exact same thing each time it appears? No! It can't! Tarot is not about learning "five easy pieces"—five facts for each card and using them over and over again. Although you may find it difficult to understand when you are beginning to learn the cards, the information I am giving you here is merely a base on which to start to add your own experience, building as you go.

THE MAJOR ARCANA

THE Major Arcana are numbered from 0 (the Fool) to 21 (the World). When viewed in this manner, the sequence is sometimes referred to as "The Fool's Journey"; that is, the cards comprise a story of the Fool on his way to enlightenment and the lessons he learns along the way. It is felt that this portion of the deck was entirely separate from the rest, and somewhere in time the two parts were joined together.

The Major Arcana ("the Majors") are considered the "trump cards" of the Tarot deck; that is, they rank higher than any suit or "pip" cards ("the Minors"). We will see that a reading with many Majors is considered a strong reading, whereas a reading with no Majors is considered weak or possibly inconclusive. This is why some people use only the Major Arcana when doing a reading. The lessons in the Major Arcana are usually karmic in scope; they do not readily respond to the intervention of us mere humans. However, nothing in Tarot is written in stone; even extreme circumstances can be utilized to achieve a satisfactory ending. This is what we will discover on our journey.

The Trumps #0–10 usually deal with questions of wants and needs. The Trumps #11–21 usually deal with questions concerning emotions and feelings.

CARD #0—THE FOOL

THE FOOL.

THIS IS A CARD ABOUT
GETTING OR MAKING
FRESH STARTS.

The Fool represents an open-minded innocent, usually the questioner (the Querent), wide-eyed and eager to learn everything he can from the world around him. He is often pictured as a well-dressed young man, but I have seen beggars and travelers on many decks. He almost always carries his belongings over his shoulder, and sometimes also a white rose, which symbolizes his spiritual desires. In this guise, he represents us all—our "inner child" as it were—ready to do, do, do! He is often accompanied by a small dog who is usually trying to get his attention, because the Fool is walking with his head up, taking in the beauty around him, and does not notice that he is about to step off a cliff! The lesson of this card is that it is okay to be a Fool, but don't be stupid! If this card turns up, it is a warning against making superficial choices. It is telling you not to have your head so far in the clouds that you forget to notice where your feet are taking you. Each of us faces many choices throughout our life; as exciting as some will appear, choose wisely when a new one is put before you.

REVERSED: When this card is reversed, think of it as the Fool having already fallen off the cliff. Bad or inappropriate choices have been made.

WORK: (Refers not only to your job, but also to enterprises, distinctions, and avocations: "that which you do.") You feel that it is time for a change; perhaps you are seeking greener pastures or looking to get out of a rut. It's never too late to try something new!

REVERSED: The grass *looks* greener, but don't believe it. Stay with what you know for the moment.

LOVE: (Refers to your emotional life, not just your sex life.) A familiar emotion makes itself known to you again. Perhaps you are hoping to form new relationships? Are you experiencing your first love infatuation?

REVERSED: Looking for love in all the wrong places? This person may not be right for you. Take a step back and try to see the whole picture.

MONEY: (Refers to material wealth, not just your finances.) New opportunities for investing make themselves known to you. Maybe this is a good time to start a wise investment program.

REVERSED: Don't spend it all in one place, even if it's burning a hole in your pocket.

FUTURE: (Consider this "strategy" or the outcome if you make no changes.) The indications are that you should go for it!

REVERSED: You are off on a wild goose chase; reconsider everything.

CARD #1—THE MAGICIAN

THE MAGICIAN.

THIS IS A CARD ABOUT ENERGY, FOCUS, AND MANIFESTATION.

The Fool's Journey: *The Magician represents intellect and creative abilities and possibilities. From the Magician, the Fool creates new opportunities and ideas. The appearance of this card tells the Querent to be creative and ingenious in dealing with problems.*

The Magician stands before a table on which rest the symbols of the four suits. Above his head is a lemniscate, the symbol of infinity, and around his waist is a snake devouring its tail—also a symbol of eternity. The Magician has one arm raised and holds his "magic wand" in his hand; he will channel energy from above to the table below, utilizing this power to achieve what he desires. He is the *channel*, not the source of his powers—and he knows that. He represents the union of Man with the Divine, which in turn gives him power and the knowledge needed to create, using the tools before him.

Some people say that he is using the wrong hand, that his left arm should be raised instead of his right. This has to do with the metaphysical theory that power is received through your left side, crosses your body, and emanates from your right (or dominant) hand. Perhaps the artist, Pamela Coleman Smith, was left-handed, or perhaps (my pet theory) she drew the image without any model, looking in a mirror with her left arm up and drawing with the pencil in her right—and that's why the image is reversed. In some newer decks, the Magician has the "correct" arm raised.

> REVERSED: When this card is reversed, think of it as the Magician's table being overturned. Without the correct tools, knowledge, or abilities to use them, nothing can be started or created. It can also indicate a waste of energy because of an inappropriate intent.

WORK: You have the capabilities; apply yourself and give it your best shot.
REVERSED: You are not achieving your full potential, or you are not being allowed to use your full potential.

LOVE: Carpe Diem!—Seize the day! Make the first move!
REVERSED: You are getting or receiving mixed messages and crossed signals. Back off at this time.

MONEY: Apply yourself: It takes money to make money. Get it working for you.
REVERSED: Money slips from your grasp; do not throw good money after bad.

FUTURE: Focus yourself and results will be realized.
REVERSED: You are using your power toward a destructive end. Projects may fail. Stop what you are doing.

CARD #2—THE HIGH PRIESTESS

THE HIGH PRIESTESS.

THIS IS A CARD ABOUT
THE INTUITIVE PROCESS.

The Fool's Journey: *The High Priestess represents the Fool's spiritual mother. In her book is all the knowledge the Fool must discover on his journey. (She may also represent the Querent's secret lover, or an unknown admirer!)*

Here we meet for the first time an image that repeats throughout the Tarot deck: a figure between two "somethings," be they trees, columns, towers, mountainsides, etc. They are generally considered to be opposites, usually positive and negative polarities (as opposed to good and evil); the figure has found the middle path between them, and in general terms, we are to do the same to achieve the qualities of the card. Also when there is a hanging veil, it usually indicates some knowledge that is currently hidden from the Querent, but it must be discovered before the next step of the journey can be taken. I will point out these images as we go along.

The High Priestess sits serenely between the two pillars of Solomon's temple—Boaz, the negative life force, and Jachin, the positive. She sits in front of a veil (virginity) decorated with pomegranates and palms (female and male symbols). Her headdress connects her, as a daughter of the Moon, to all moon goddesses, and to the Virgin Mary. She holds a Torah (Tora) of sacred laws, but her veil covers part of it, indicating that there are things the Querent has yet to learn. In a man's reading, she may represent the perfect woman he seeks; in a woman's reading, it may indicate virtues in a friend or in herself.

The High Priestess represents intuition, hidden knowledge, spiritual enlightenment, and inner illumination. She knows the secrets and wishes to share them with you, but there is one catch—you have to ask her first. She will willingly give you the knowledge you seek, but she does not give it freely to just anyone. There is a metaphysical theory that states all knowledge is to be found within us and we have the answers to all our questions if only we will seek our own counsel. Perhaps intuition, the sudden "flash" of understanding that makes everything crystal clear, is but our mind's use of this process.

If we perceive that the High Priestess does not represent the Querent, she may stand for someone the Querent trusts without reservation.

REVERSED: When this card is reversed, think that the veils have covered the High Priestess's face and things are unclear for the moment. It may indicate a time when no clear answers are available or perhaps there is only false counsel.

WORK: New things are happening and new plans are being made; go with your gut feelings.
REVERSED: Promises, promises! Some made in the past may never be kept or may be forgotten.

LOVE: When your head fails, go with your heart.
REVERSED: It's not your head or heart—it's your hormones doing the talking.

MONEY: A change in finances or income improves your bankbook balances.
REVERSED: Financial reversals from unseen problems.

FUTURE: Prepare well, consider well, but act prudently. Do not allow anything to escape your scrutiny.
REVERSED: Indulgence, conceit, or superficial knowledge influences a major decision.

CARD #3—THE EMPRESS

THE EMPRESS.

THIS IS A CARD ABOUT
PROGRESS AND
PRODUCTIVITY.

The Fool's Journey: *The Empress represents the security and guidance of parents, a happy and mature relationship, Mother energy—maybe pregnancy!*

There are several cards in the Tarot deck that some feel are a sure sign of pregnancy; this is one of them! *Warning!* Practically as well as ethically, I feel it is wrong to discuss pregnancy or death (more about that later) in the context of a Tarot reading. Yes, this card may *indicate* pregnancy, but that should *not* be something you impart to a Querent! You could be very, very mistaken!

The Empress sits in the middle of abundance—usually a field of wheat or under a grape arbor, symbols of material abundance—after a period of waiting. The Empress is usually pictured as being quite pregnant, symbolizing fertility. Marriage, balance, stability, and contentment are all indicated by this card; something has been labored over and planned for, and is now coming to fruition—whether it be a marriage, harvest, work project, kitchen remodeling, or what-have-you. This card is about the realization of the proposed outcome. The shield sometimes seen at her side bears the symbol of Venus. (Her counterpart, the Emperor, bears the symbol of Mars.)

Most people feel that the Earth Mother qualities of this card can represent the Querent's own mother, for she is a very nurturing individual.

REVERSED: When this card is reversed, think of plans coming to a fruitless end, or the desired outcome being disrupted in a negative way. The result could include infidelity, poverty, or even war!

WORK: Your plans are moving forward; even if it looks like things might take a longer time than expected before you see the pay-off, progress is still being made.
REVERSED: Growth is slower than expected and might come to a halt. Hang in there and hope for the best, but hope may be all you can do.

LOVE: Expect the best and it will come to you.
REVERSED: Infertility, menopause problems, a wedding postponed. That spark will never become a flaming passion.

MONEY: Tend each asset wisely; one is about to pay off.
REVERSED: Expected growth does not take place.

FUTURE: Everything is being done according to your plan. Be patient—the harvest is about to begin.
REVERSED: Things you have hoped for will not develop as rapidly or as fully as you have expected.

CARD #4—THE EMPEROR

THE EMPEROR.

THIS IS A CARD ABOUT THE USES OF POWER AND POWER STRUCTURES. IT CAN REPRESENT SOME-ONE WHO DOES WELL IN A HIGHLY STRUCTURED ENVIRONMENT.

The Fool's Journey: *From the Emperor, the Fool learns the need for wisdom and for leadership, law, and order. It is a card about Father energy.*

A very warlike card! The Emperor sits on a throne surrounded by symbols of Mars, the god of war. Under his robes he wears a full suit of armor as though he will be ready at a moment's notice to defend his kingdom and his people. He *is* authority; in him are reason, government, leadership, and paternity. He can be seen as a general in the armed forces, or at least a commanding officer. (Some readers feel that he represents a woman's intended, but I don't think most people would find that very appealing!)

The Emperor can also represent the Querent's father. Despite his warlike exterior, the Emperor is full of knowledge and deeply caring. He can also represent other male authority figures, such as a judge in a lawsuit, the police, the dean of a college, the loan officer at your bank, but most times it may turn out to be your boss! The appearance of this card might indicate that you will be having an audience with someone higher up on the corporate ladder.

Although this card usually represents another person in the Querent's life, it can also represent a male Querent, if he is the commanding type, very sure of himself, or if he feels he is the captain of his own destiny. The Emperor can also represent an institution, such as a bank or a court, rather than a specific individual.

REVERSED: When this card is reversed, think of someone who is out-of-control, immature, cranky, or weak-willed. It can indicate corporate turmoil or downsizing, or a judgment being made that will negatively impact you, even if it was not made directly about you.

WORK: Rules, procedures, standards, and policies are involved; you are expected to comply, and give your top performance.
REVERSED: You are going to have to explain and account for everything you've done so far.

LOVE: Someone wants or has the controlling hand in this relationship. I rarely see this card pop up in a love relationship reading.
REVERSED: What might have been a one-sided relationship seems to be working out for the better.

(Note: Here is an example of a reversed card having a more positive meaning than the upright one. A common mistake people make is thinking that upright cards are "good" and reversed cards are "bad." When we get to the number Five pip cards, you may see that the opposite is true. Always assume the most positive thing you can in a reading. A reversed Emperor might indicate that the Querent is better off *out* of this relationship.)

MONEY: Your financial state needs planning to reinforce it. Seek wise counsel before making any definite plans or changes, no matter how minor.
REVERSED: Your finances are going to be scrutinized as never before. This indicates possible losses from bad investing, and definitely bad counsel has been given.

FUTURE: The best offense is a good defense. Trust someone in power to look out for you or at least point you in the right direction.
REVERSED: You'd better have eyes in the back of your head if you plan to let your guard down.

CARD #5—THE HIEROPHANT

THIS IS A CARD ABOUT
PRINCIPLES AND
CONFORMITY;
MAINTAINING THE
STATUS QUO.

The Fool's Journey: *The Hierophant represents the Querent's spiritual father and/or someone he highly respects. From the Hierophant, the Fool learns humility and compassion.*

Here is another figure between two objects—this time the two columns represent duality. There are two crossed keys—a gold one (the sun and the superconscious) and a silver one (the moon and the unconscious)—and two acolytes, one with robes decorated with white roses or lilies (abstract thought) and one with the red roses of desire. This red-and-white flower symbolism also trails throughout the Tarot.

The Hierophant appears very much like the Christian Pope in full regalia. He might represent an actual person, a particular institution, or a way of thinking. The Hierophant is ruled by the conventional, and conventional it must be. He feels: "Why should we change anything? It has always worked this way and it always will." It is this stagnation in thought that holds him back. He refuses to change in the face of new (and possibly great) events.

Tradition and orthodoxy are the key to his future. Some people or institutions (religious or otherwise) feel this need to conform for social approval—or at the very least so they don't lose their funding. Some people like to have their thinking done for them. For some, the prospect of facing something new is frightening.

> REVERSED: When this card is reversed, think of the social order of things collapsing. It says you are unconventional or unorthodox, which can be negative or positive. This is the card of rebellious youth but also the card of the inventor. Maybe it's time to start thinking for yourself; your beliefs are holding you back.

WORK: Make a leap of faith; someone above is looking out for you. Perhaps your boss is thinking about having a conference with you.
REVERSED: The rumor mill is cranking full force; don't believe everything you hear through the grapevine.

LOVE: Take a stand! Commit to something. Believe in something. The Hierophant can also represent your lover's parents, who want to speak with the two of you about your relationship.
REVERSED: Ask to be forgiven; learn to forget. It may also represent parental interference or objection to your relationship.

MONEY: Time to add money to an office pool; you may be asked to contribute money to a worthy cause, or maybe just someone's bridal shower. Perhaps you should see your banker about better investments.
REVERSED: Be careful or your money could come up short this month.

FUTURE: Expect help to come from traditional means. Give it your best shot, even if the opportunity comes at the very last second. Perhaps you need to seek counsel.
REVERSED: Be prepared to hold on until the bitter end; that may be all you can do to get the results you were expecting.

CARD #6—THE LOVERS

THE LOVERS.

> THIS IS A CARD ABOUT (PHYSICAL) UNITY, BUT IT GOES BEYOND THE CONCEPT OF A "SIGNIFICANT OTHER."

The Fool's Journey: Decisions! Decisions! The Fool is warned to make wise choices, for an unwise decision could have far-reaching consequences.

The original drawing of this card and its concept were quite different in the old decks. Cupid (now replaced by the archangel Raphael, Angel of the Air) flew overhead, while either a young man or an old man stood between and/or embraced two women, one fair (representing the intellectual) and one dark (representing the sensual). So, maybe you're wondering what the modern decks—showing two naked people and an angel—have to do with making choices!

The first reaction a Querent may have to this card is that it represents a current or future love relationship. It can, but most comments about the workings or dysfunction of one's love life are usually found in the pip cards, particularly in the Cups, which deal with emotions. Later on, compare this card with the Two of Cups, which is about cementing relationships, including business partnerships. Also, compare this couple to the one in the Devil, #15 (15 = 1 + 5 = 6, the Lovers).

Here the man, representing conscious mind and reason, looks

to the woman, representing the unconscious mind and emotions. It is she who is looking up at the angel of the superconscious. The really *deep* metaphysical explanation is that it is almost impossible to reach the superconscious with the conscious mind. It can only be reached by way of the unconscious mind through meditation or prayer, representing love undisturbed by material desires. It can indicate the beginnings of romance. It may also reveal the beginnings of temptation.

You are wondering what this card has to do with decisions. Putting the above philosophical discussion aside, this card is about the harmony between one's inner and outer life, also harmony usually achieved through the presence of another individual. In my concept of "twos" (yes, the number of the Lovers card is six, but the couple represents a "two"), a two represents duality, the pairing of opposites, and even creativity unfulfilled. The male cannot reach the higher stages he desires without the intervention of the female.

REVERSED: When this card is reversed, think of the expulsion of Adam and Eve from paradise, the fall from grace. It may indicate a time of physical separation, emotional drift, or plain loneliness. It suggests infidelity, interference, or wrong choices.

WORK: An offer of employment is extended or renewed; possibly a workplace love interest.
REVERSED: Handing in your resignation? Business and pleasure do not mix well.

LOVE: Someone pops the question, and the expected answer is given.
REVERSED: Love on the rebound, wishful (or lustful) thinking; a "crush" comes to an end.

MONEY: This might be a good time to combine your resources— just read all the fine print. Don't be afraid to ask for a prenuptial agreement.
REVERSED: That "deal on a handshake" dries up. Security disintegrates. Assets are no longer considered "joint."

FUTURE: A partnering is in the offing: charm, tact, and a sense of diplomacy will be involved.
REVERSED: Beware: someone is hiding something from you.

CARD #7—THE CHARIOT

THE CHARIOT.

THIS IS A CARD ABOUT
FORCES IN OPPOSITION;
CONFLICT AND ITS
RESOLUTION ARE
INVOLVED.

The Fool's Journey: *This card deals with decisions in the present. After digesting the lessons of the tutors on his journey, the Fool comes face to face with this dynamic card and feels the inner turmoil of opposing desires. He cannot progress until his own conflicts are resolved.*

After the calm teachings of the previous cards, this card stands out! The Charioteer rides forth pulled by two sphinxes (or unicorns, or lions). Once again they are black and white: the black a symbol of stern justice, the white a symbol of mercy. These two opposing forces pull the chariot forward, but they also pull against each other in an attempt to tear the Charioteer asunder, and it is the Charioteer's job to keep them under his control at all times or suffer the consequences. Although he may be filled with inner turmoil over this, outwardly he is calm and confident. The Charioteer is usually pictured under a starry canopy of some sort, indicating that he is under celestial influences that will affect his victory. The sphinxes are a reference to the Society of the Golden Dawn. Both Waite and Smith were members.

This is a card about success, victory achieved after hard work, and a well-balanced life. (There's the figure between the two black and white objects again.) This card indicates victory for someone who has held control and has conquered the forces of emotion and the mind. It can also indicate recovery after an illness, moving and travel plans, and perhaps even a new car!

> REVERSED: When this card is reversed, think that the opposing forces have flipped the Chariot over and all forward motion has stopped. Maybe the stakes are too high, or a truce is only temporary. This may indicate an unethical victory, an unbalanced life, or may be an indication of pending illness. (Once again, I would never go as far to say it indicates that people are going to get sick or hurt, but suggest that Querents be more careful in taking chances, or more sensible with their diet. Do not plant seeds of negativity in the Querents' mind!)

WORK: A leader emerges from the ranks; a conflict is finally resolved to your mutual satisfaction and benefit.
REVERSED: Your expected promotion or raise is delayed and may not take place after all.

LOVE: You are winning (or being won over) in a battle of the heart. Don't lose control.
REVERSED: Crash and burn time: someone you thought was true has just made you another entry on the scorecard.

MONEY: Triumph at last! Creating an attack plan gives you control over your finances. Be aware of interest rates and penalties.
REVERSED: In spite of your best efforts, it seems as though you are not getting ahead any time soon. Car troubles cost big bucks.

FUTURE: Put your best face on, your best foot forward. Chances are good right now for just about anything.
REVERSED: You have just allowed yourself to be run over roughshod. Accept this defeat and wait for the balance of power to restore itself.

CARD #8—STRENGTH

The Fool's Journey: *Fresh on the heels of the dynamic Charioteer, the Fool meets a powerful force of a much different kind—an enchantress with charms—and the Fool learns that self-discipline is vital! It is a warning to be self-controlled and to practice restraint.*

This card has changed many times throughout the years. Some older decks show a man (Hercules or Samson?) subduing a lion by brute force. The concept was that physical strength would overcome all obstacles—that the Querent is trying to *make* something happen by determination and will. Some of the old decks call this card "Fortitude," probably from *Sforza*—Italian for "strength."

The Rider-Waite deck is quite different: a woman is *closing* a lion's mouth, showing that applying love and consideration is the best way to handle a situation. She has no physical strength to speak of. The lemniscate over her head (as in the Magician) shows her connection to the powers of the Universe, since she is a highly developed spiritual being. By tapping into the power of the Higher Self, she can overcome a threat though spiritual strength instead of brute force. This is also a card for people who act instinctively and intuitively, or relate well to animals, such as a veterinarian.

This card says love is stronger than hate.

In some decks, card #8 is *Justice* and card #11 is *Strength*. Waite changed the numbering to fit into his ideas and system of doing things; also because the lion represents Leo, and Waite associates Leo with the number eight.

> REVERSED: When reversed, think of this card as the lion regaining control; this card shows discord in one's life, possibly the Querent having given too much attention to the material instead of the spiritual. Perhaps it says that in the past the Querent handled things badly, was destructive with a passion, or acted without regard to others. It is a warning to reach for the spiritual side of things. The reversal can also mean you are sending or receiving crossed signals or mixed messages.

WORK: You passed a test; a challenging assignment is completed successfully. You achieved an end without stooping to an elaborate show of force.

REVERSED: You bit off more than you could chew, but rather than stand and oppose something you dislike, you run to the nearest hiding place.

LOVE: Be gentle in everything you do; loving someone does not mean controlling him or her.

REVERSED: Someone is bringing you down because he or she refuses to listen to you or respect your feelings; perhaps an abusive relationship is indicated.

MONEY: Your investments are sound; all the loose ends are neatly tied up. Creature comforts are fine, but beware of becoming a collector of possessions or feeling that they declare your worth to others.

REVERSED: Overspending on luxuries may be getting out of control; modify your purchasing behaviors.

FUTURE: A spirit of fair play and optimism will get you through the day; cooperate.

REVERSED: Indicates a misuse of power or trust. Someone is trying too hard to make a point.

CARD #9—THE HERMIT

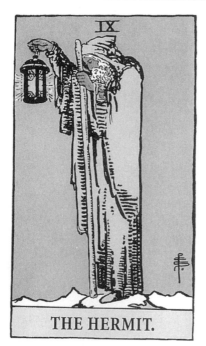

THIS IS A CARD ABOUT
SEEKING ONE'S OWN
TRUTH, AND ABOUT THE
TEACHING AND THE
LEARNING OF LESSONS.

The Fool's Journey: *From the Hermit, the Fool learns the value of solitary reflection. The Fool finds that he needs to take the time to stop and think and ponder on his journey and the teachers he has met.*

We have all read about people who retreated from life and other people, and sought to "find the answer" or to "find themselves." The concept of leaving the material behind and seeking the spiritual is a popular theme for "vision questers," but it can have mixed results, depending on the individual's state of mind. (Compare Jesus' 40-day fast in the desert to Theodore [The Unabomber] Kaczynski's "manifesto.") This is a card about seeking wisdom, either directly from another, or from meditation and reflection upon the writing of others, or our attempts to "go within."

The Hermit stands alone on a snowy mountaintop (he *is* on a mountaintop, if you look closely) with a lantern (of Truth) in hand. He has found his answer and is "casting light" for the next person to climb up the mountain. In one deck, the climber's face can be seen in the corner of the card, and it is a younger version of the Hermit's face. The Hermit is at the height of his spiritual wisdom and lights the way for those who are willing to listen to him. This is the card of the teacher or counselor, one with a gentle wisdom, someone willing to help guide without imposing his own system of beliefs on yours.

The person indicated can be a guidance counselor, a therapist, a financial consultant, the human resources department, the rector of your church, or the principal of the high school—someone with wisdom to impart. It can also be *you*—the person others seek out when they are in need—don't disregard that possibility.

REVERSED: When reversed, think that the Hermit has slipped off his mountaintop and the lantern has gone out, which can indicate a few different things. It may be a warning against false counsel, someone deliberately misleading you; it can also indicate that the message you received is not what you wanted to hear. Usually, however, it indicates that a lack of maturity is present. The Querent either refuses the wisdom of others or spurns it in an attempt to prove that he or she doesn't need advice. It can indicate that the Querent is involved in foolish or dangerous vices, or is living in a childish world and refuses to grow up.

WORK: Get a second opinion; seek advice from an old hand. Think something through before acting on it.
REVERSED: The future is uncertain; progress is not being made or is being prevented.

LOVE: A period of abstinence begins or ends. You may feel like a celibate hermit, but perhaps that is the lesson for the moment.
REVERSED: A loved one is delayed; your "lonely hearts" advisor throws no light on your problems.

MONEY: Make better use of the financial assets you have been assembling all this time; maybe even divest or dispose of them after careful consideration.
REVERSED: You are heading for financial ruin; do not throw good money after bad.

FUTURE: You will gain a new perspective by getting away for a while. Retreat, hide out, or lie low until things change or look better to you. Inaction may be the right tack to take.
REVERSED: Delays are caused by trying to be too careful in spite of good advice. Also can indicate that someone is lying to you. See what the surrounding cards indicate.

CARD #10—THE WHEEL OF FORTUNE

WHEEL of FORTUNE.

═══
THIS IS A CARD ABOUT
LUCK; CHANCE AND
CHANGE ARE INVOLVED.
═══

The Fool's Journey: *Good and bad news! The Fool discovers that everyone encounters changes in circumstance no matter how well they planned. It is no good blaming misfortunes on "fate"—it is more important to make the best of what cannot be changed.*

The Wheel of Fortune keeps on turning and carries humans and their destinies up and then down. On one pagan-theme deck there is pictured the concept of Maiden-Mother-Crone; on one old deck four figures carry banners that say: "I shall reign," "I reign," "I have reigned," and "I am without reign." It indicates the unexpected arrival of good fortune and success. It also indicates that everything happens in a cycle or circle, and in its own time. Upright, this card is always accepted as being the harbinger of good luck and good fortune.

It is also a card filled with odd and peculiar symbolism, including a snake, a demon, and a Sphinx. The number four occurs several times on this card. There are four mystical creatures in the corners of the card (also repeated in Card #21—The World). They are an angel, which also represents the element of Air and the astrological sign Aquarius; an eagle, representing Water and Scorpio; a winged lion representing Fire and Leo; and a winged bull representing Earth and Taurus. They are the four fixed signs of the Zodiac and they are also associated with the four gospels of the New Testament. (Figure out that connection!)

There are also the letters **T**, **A**, **R**, **O** (T-A-R-O-T if you start and end with the 'T') interspersed with IHVH for Jehovah. All of this is supposed to show that spiritual reality is unchanging, though the wheel ("rota") of your personal life keeps turning. (In this card, you may notice that Tarot, taro, rota, and Tora [the sacred scroll the High Priestess holds] are an anagram. Thus: "rota" = wheel, "taro" = road, "tora" = law.)

> REVERSED: When this card is reversed, the Wheel is turned and dumps all the figures on their heads. Luck has deserted the Querent; there will be setbacks, and it will seem as though everything is wrong with the world. Courage will be required to overcome this difficulty, but a good reader will focus on the facing of challenges, on their part in character development, and on the need to keep moving forward.

WORK: Changes will be made that give you a chance to climb up the corporate ladder. Expect things to go your way.
REVERSED: "Boom" will quickly turn into "bust."

LOVE: A relationship may not last forever, but it will be a good thing as long as it lasts.
REVERSED: A hot romance heads for the cooler quickly.

MONEY: The market is guaranteed to fluctuate—find a good financial advisor before taking any risks!
REVERSED: Gut feelings and hunches fail to pay off.

FUTURE: Minimize your risk by preparing well. Leave room for escape (or an escape clause) when moving into uncertain territory.
REVERSED: Nothing ventured, nothing gained. (Remember, getting a negative card does not guarantee that is the only outcome. Quite realistically, getting this card in reverse could be saying you refuse to take risks and therefore lose out on possible opportunities.)

CARD #11—JUSTICE

THIS IS A CARD ABOUT
WEIGHING EVIDENCE,
JUDGMENT, AND
DECISION MAKING; NOT
RESTRICTED TO
LEGAL MATTERS

The Fool's Journey: *The Fool meets his next challenge—the Underworld. Here the Fool encounters the darkest and most ominous cards in the Tarot. If the first section of the Major Arcana is considered "The Fool Begins His Journey," this next section can be considered "The Fool Goes to Hell." Justice suggests solutions for the Fool's dilemmas. The Fool learns the value of reason, wisdom, and considered argument. There can be legal solutions that may not be as straightforward as they seem.*

Justice sits before a veil suspended between two columns. Have we seen this image before? Not only does Justice bear a strong resemblance to the High Priestess, but they are also linked in numerology (11 = 1 + 1 = 2, the number of the High Priestess)! This is not blind justice; she sits with her eyes open to see all that is going on and make her judgments accordingly. In her right hand she holds a sword; in her left she holds scales to ensure that her decision is just. Note that all swords in Tarot are two-sided, meaning that they can cut both ways.

The appearance of this card overwhelmingly says "judge and

legal system." It may represent the judge in a legal case, the lawyers, or even the lawsuit itself. Justice may be done, although that may *not* be the outcome the Querent desires. However, it may also indicate a good outcome to a pending lawsuit with both parties satisfied. A good reader will not give any definite meaning to this card without first reading the cards that surround it to get a better picture of the sequence of events. The overall meaning of the card is about "balanced judgment." It describes a person who is a logical or analytical thinker, or someone who enforces or upholds the law. A balanced personality demands that one get rid of prejudices and preconceptions.

> REVERSED: Think that Justice has become unsettled and the scales are out of balance. This can indicate legal complications, injustice, inequality, or the loss of a lawsuit. It may also indicate a biased mind full of prejudice, be it the judge, the one bringing the lawsuit, or just the Querent going about his or her daily business. Once again, the card has to do with making decisions, not necessarily legal ones. How often do we have to make snap decisions and hope we have made a wise choice!

WORK: Know the rules! Your job performance is being reviewed or documented.
REVERSED: Time off is denied. The rules seem to get bent for everyone else but not for you.

LOVE: Openness and honesty are called for. The truth, the whole truth, and nothing but the truth!
REVERSED: A past indiscretion is revealed. You may have to explain something you'd rather forget than recall.

MONEY: Weigh the alternatives: pros and cons are involved. Balance your checkbook.
REVERSED: Your bills get paid late or payments made do not get received on time.

FUTURE: You are responsible for your own actions; consider the consequences.
REVERSED: Be careful whom you trust; true intentions are not being revealed at this time.

CARD #12—THE HANGED MAN

THE HANGED MAN.

THIS IS A CARD ABOUT CROSSROADS AND TRANSITIONS. IT DESCRIBES PEOPLE WHO THINK ABOUT THEIR PAST ACTIONS, TRY TO IMPROVE THEMSELVES, OR WHO CAREFULLY CONSIDER THEIR NEXT MOVE.

The Fool's Journey: *Disillusionment—the Fool learns to question values and search for new solutions when things no longer make sense. The appearance of the card suggests that sacrifices may be needed and the Fool should try looking at the world from a different perspective.*

This is one of the many "cards of change" that we will meet as we go through the deck. And it is a strange card, indeed. The Hanged Man is hanging from one ankle, not from his neck. There is no concept of torture or punishment attached to his "hanging"; his face is serene and untroubled, and we are not sure if his hands are bound or not. In some decks the man is hanging by his knee over a branch and no bindings are indicated. Some artists place a nimbus or halo around his head. No hangman's gallows are indicated; in fact, he is hanging from a living tree. So, what's going on in this card?

Self-surrender to a higher wisdom—maybe even a desire for spiritual enlightenment is here. The presence of this card can indicate someone who has a gift of prophecy or clairvoyance, and uses it for good if the card is upright. (Upright means he's upside down, remember!)

As a card of change it is about *stasis*—a time for reflection. Unlike other cards of change, such as Death or the Tower, where the change is swift, this change is coming slowly. Also, unlike the other cards where there is nothing you can do but wait and accept, the Hanged Man is being given a unique opportunity—a chance to contemplate and make choices that will affect the outcome of the change. By hanging upside down he is being given a chance to "look at things differently," being given a change of perspective. This card says to take a good look around and see where you've been and where you are going, and to choose wisely. Rarely will life give you such opportunities! A maturation process is indicated.

REVERSED: Think that the Hanged Man is no longer hanging but standing on the ground. This means he may be absorbed by the physical or preoccupied with concerns of the self and not guided by the wisdom of others. It may mean he hasn't time—or doesn't want time—to learn that he has a soul. If this person has a gift such as clairvoyance, reversal may indicate that he or she is using it for selfish gains or personal motives and is "blinded" to the change, being "grounded" in the physical.

WORK: Perhaps it is time to stop and to reconsider trying something different instead of hanging in there with no plan in mind.
REVERSED: If you are going to work without plans, don't forget a safety net!

LOVE: You must decide something about and for yourself, even if in a relationship.
REVERSED: You are listening to your hormones instead of thinking things through.

MONEY: Changes in spending, investing, and saving money are involved. Cutbacks may be in order, so think every move through.
REVERSED: Stop guessing and seek the advice of financial professionals.

FUTURE: Apply your experience to get out of a current deadlock. Sit and think awhile.
REVERSED: You are refusing the counsel and wisdom of others and are boldly going nowhere fast.

CARD #13—DEATH

DEATH.

THIS CARD *DOES NOT* PREDICT DEATH FOR THE QUERENT OR FOR ANY PERSON HE OR SHE KNOWS.

The Fool's Journey: *Faced with Death, the Fool learns that Death does not bring an end—only change. The Fool learns not to be frightened of change but to embrace the challenge of a new order.*

Here we have one of the most frightening cards for your Querent to see: in bold letters it says "DEATH"—how would you expect them to react? Death on horseback tramples a once-fertile field and all peoples great and small bow down before him. Usually the Death figure carries a five-petal white rose—a symbol of the life force. What the card really means is that everything is in constant circulation; the life force comes to materialization and flows out again in a continuing pattern.

Here we have yet another card of change, a change that is coming and will be here in time. It is a card about the destruction of the old, followed by the birth or rebirth of the new. It can refer to patterns in your life—prejudices, values, and beliefs—anything that will gradually die and be replaced by new ideals and hopes (which in their turn may get discarded, too). The point is that you cannot stop this change; it will be better for you to embrace what follows (it may be even *better* than what preceded it) than to despair over the change. The mere presence of this card in *no way* signals disaster—unless reversed.

The image of the card has changed radically—from a skeleton reaping heads to a beautiful crimson-robed hooded figure gesturing for you to follow him. One deck eliminated the card completely and replaced it with a card called "Transition."

> REVERSED: When this card is reversed and Death has been thrown from the horse's back, an important change has been stalled. Then the card indicates stagnation or inertia, political unrest, and impending disaster.

WORK: Changes shake up the workplace for the good. The surrounding cards will indicate whether it is for the good of the company or of the individual.
REVERSED: Have a current resume available.

LOVE: This card does not bode well in love relationships. A point of departure has been reached—say your good-byes.
REVERSED: This relationship will only bring more heartache and worries. Go while the going is good.

MONEY: Add up your current assets and liabilities and then launch new financial plans. A possible inheritance.
REVERSED: Put your money in more stable places before it's lost.

FUTURE: Prepare a fresh canvas for yourself and clear out the past. Expect something good to happen.
REVERSED: This is not the time to make any large purchases or extensive future plans.

CARD #14—TEMPERANCE

TEMPERANCE.

THIS IS A CARD ABOUT
DYNAMICS AND BALANCE.
IT DESCRIBES PEOPLE
WHO INSTINCTIVELY
KNOW HOW TO PUT
SOMETHING TOGETHER
(INVENTORS, COOKS,
CRAFTSPERSONS).

The Fool's Journey: *The Fool discovers a balance between heart and mind that he needs to thread his way through the temptations and trials of the Underworld.*

You are probably asking: "If the Fool is on his way to Hell, what's the angel doing here?" Well, many of us have asked that question, and the best answer I can give is that the archangel Michael pops in to offer hope to the Fool that the trials of Hell will lead to enlightenment, if he doesn't lose heart. The lesson of this card is "All things in moderation—*including* moderation!"

The title Temperance has more to do with the tempering of two opposite qualities than rejecting the evils of alcohol. A figure stands with one foot on land and one in water (we will see this imagery again soon), indicating a balance between the material and the spiritual. Some figures have a triangle within a square on their breast, a symbol of matter ascending into spirit. The figure is pouring the essence of life from a silver goblet to a golden one (or something similar—I've even seen the figure juggling gold and silver balls instead) and back again, signifying the entry of spirit into matter, blending the conscious and the unconscious.

This is a card about adaptation, utilizing self-control, working in harmony with others; also good management and a sound outlook on life, learning to find the balance point. It also means that the Querent is able to put together successful combinations of things—from business partnerships, to matchmaking, to being a good cook or bartender! However, this card sometimes requires great struggles or personal sacrifice. Although it can indicate that a difficult period is about to end, it *does not* necessarily mean that the Querent will like the results, but all that can be done has been done.

Sometimes to achieve this balance, compromises have to be made, and sometimes compromise means that no one is completely happy. The road to enlightenment is not always a smooth one.

> REVERSED: When Temperance is reversed, it indicates bad management, poor judgment, competing business interests, that the Querent is not good at successfully putting things together, or that the combinations may be evil (intentionally or otherwise). It says that the Querent is out of balance or extreme in his or her passions.

WORK: Create new order out of chaos; be creative and employ new strategies.
REVERSED: Be careful of those around you. Someone may be trying to use "divide and conquer" techniques.

LOVE: What starts as a purely physical attraction develops into a long-lasting relationship.
REVERSED: A love affair was too hot not to cool down.

MONEY: Turn a hobby into a moneymaking venture. Refinance. Channel funds for higher yields.
REVERSED: Think twice about investing in this project.

FUTURE: Mix and match! Use existing components to find something bigger and better.
REVERSED: Oil and water do not mix. Rethink before you act.

CARD #15—THE DEVIL

THE DEVIL.

THIS IS A CARD ABOUT
BONDAGE OR
ENTRAPMENT. IT
DESCRIBES SOMEONE
WHO FEELS HELPLESS,
OPPRESSED, OR CANNOT
SEE THE WAY OUT OF A
BAD SITUATION.

The Fool's Journey: *A new challenge—enslavement to evil. The Fool realizes we all have a dark side that must be overcome.*

If people hassle you about Tarot being "The Devil's Picture Book," they will certainly point to this card as "proof." Tarot readers do not worship the devil any more than having a picture of Cher indicates that you worship her. The "devil" is a Western concept and the figure pictured is a Christian devil, or Satan.

The mere appearance of this card in a reading is thought to indicate that unfortunate circumstances are about to occur, or that the Querent is in immediate danger or under a threat.

The Devil figure squats on a half-block, signifying half-knowledge of the truth. He holds a torch upside down as a torch of destruction, not the light of knowledge. His right hand is upraised in what is supposed to be a sign of black magic. On his brow is an inverted star, indicating that Man's place in the cosmos is reversed and that his intentions are evil. The two nude figures echo those of #6, The Lovers (and numerically are linked: $15 - 1 + 5 = 6$). They are chained to the block of half-knowledge.

The card deals with greed, temptation, illness, perversity, and bondage to the material and to the wrong ideals. There may be a disregard for human dignity and a domination of matter over spirit. It can indicate a weak person with a tendency to indecision or being ineffective, or those who refuse to stand up for themselves, believing that "the devil we know is better than the one we don't know." The chains the couple wears are chains of their own making, like Jacob Marley's comment: "It is the chain I forged in life, link by link."

> REVERSED: When reversed, take a look at those chains; they are loose and could slip right off. The couple could simply walk away. Evil influences have been resisted or overcome. A decision to "break the chains that bind" has been made.

WORK: If you think you can get ahead in this job, think again, and get out fast.
REVERSED: Update those resumes and keep looking for a better job, which *is* out there.

LOVE: You are being used; someone wants to control you—get out while you can.
REVERSED: A bad relationship gets out of hand and ends—good riddance!

MONEY: Materialism has sucked you in so far that you almost can't see daylight. Learn how to dig yourself out and do it quickly.
REVERSED: You can't take it with you; look for the spiritual things in life.

FUTURE: Get it in writing, then read the fine print. Are there penalties for early withdrawals?
REVERSED: Stand up for your rights and be counted as a person.

CARD #16—THE TOWER

THE TOWER.

THIS IS A CARD ABOUT CATASTROPHIC CHANGE. YOU CAN EXPECT TO BE SHOCKED INTO YOUR SENSES OR WITNESS A SHOCKING EVENT WITHOUT WARNING. THE QUERENT WILL BE THRUST INTO NEW CIRCUMSTANCES WITH NO IDEA OF THE RESULTS.

The Fool's Journey: *The shattering of old illusions brings a period of momentous change. The Fool is forced to seek new philosophies upon which to rebuild.*

Also known as The Tower of God and The Tower of Destruction, this card consistently signifies bad news, even more so than #15, The Devil card, and contrasts well with the next card, The Star. A tower, being battered by a raging storm (and in some decks also by a raging sea), appears ready to crumble when a sudden lightning strike shears the top off the tower, throwing its hapless inhabitants to their destruction. As a card of change, it is certainly the most drastic! Not only is the change coming or already here, but it will come so hard and fast that you cannot even prepare for it, nor for what will come after the change.

This card can mean anything—from selfish ambition coming to naught, to bankruptcy, divorce, and the overthrow of an existing way of life, to pride going before a fall, to conflict and disruption. The tower represents ambition; the crown materialistic thought. The tower built on shaky ground or with shoddy methods most certainly will come tumbling down. You can warn the Querent, but little can be done to stop it.

What *positive* spin can be put on this card? If it falls near a card of travel, Querents may get a change of residence and a fresh start, if they mend their ways. A Court card nearby may indicate the person responsible for the downfall. A spiritual card following it may show that they have learned their lesson.

REVERSED: When reversed, this card does not read much better. It can indicate all of the previous meanings, but to a lesser degree. Freedom of mind or body may be gained, but at great cost. False accusations may be brought against the Querent, even false imprisonment.

WORK: Someone wants to make sure you get the message—and/or a pink slip.
REVERSED: Feelings of helplessness from computer systems "going down," work or school delayed from large storms or power outages.

LOVE: The breakup of a relationship or marriage; it most definitely indicates the process will not be simple or private. Interestingly, someone told me once that The Tower indicates a red-hot love affair with sparks flying and the earth moving! It would depend on the surrounding cards, of course!
REVERSED: A falling out leaves you confused and on your own.

MONEY: Be on the alert! Let that money burn a hole in your pocket. Make sure you have enough insurance and that your 401K is not building someone else a vacation home in Aruba.
REVERSED: Be cautious where electronics and your money meet, such as ATMs, online shopping, or loaning a charge card.

FUTURE: Unless you think fast, loss and destruction are distinct possibilities. The situation is about to explode in your face or collapse in upon itself.
REVERSED: Always have a Plan B ready; do not fail to create a back-up system for your electronic files.

CARD #17—THE STAR

THE STAR.

THIS IS A CARD ABOUT
CONNECTION WITH THE
COSMOS; IT DESCRIBES
PEOPLE WHO HAVE GREAT
HOPES, LIVE UP TO THEIR
HIGHEST POTENTIAL, OR
WHO ARE PARTICULARLY
WELL-SUITED TO THEIR
ENVIRONMENT.

The Fool's Journey: *Strengthened by his trials in the Underworld, the Fool emerges from his journey with a glimmer of hope. The Star suggests new opportunities and a new start.*

Climbing out of Hell, the Fool gets a glimpse of Heaven. He knows he still has a ways to go but is moving towards his destination. A beautiful maiden is kneeling with one foot on land and one in water (similar to Temperance, #14), symbolizing her balance between matter (dry land) and the unconscious (water). Whereas Temperance mixed the waters of life, in this card they are poured back into the pool with impartiality and onto the earth, where some artists show them splitting into five rivulets for the five senses. The large bird on the tree of the mind is supposed to be the "sacred ibis" of thought. Eight stars with eight points appear in the sky representing radiant cosmic energy. The number eight represents the potential for success (1 + 7 = 8). The understanding is that a positive change of mind, fortitude, and the reaching of equilibrium from the Power Within will be necessary to achieve the change, but the card is imbued with success, not failure.

This card contrasts vividly with the pessimism of the previous card (The Tower) since it consistently represents good news and optimism. Even if the reading contains some problematic future cards, this card falling in a future placement tells the Querent to rely on those who helped in the past, and to hope for the best even if caution is necessary at the moment. The appearance of this card says that health will improve, new friendships will develop, old ones will deepen, and unselfish aid will be given. This is a card that says, "You can't lose!"

Yes, it does have a downside.

REVERSED: When this card is reversed, it indicates that the Querent is pessimistic about everything—with or without just cause. In fact, it may indicate that the answer is plain and easy to see, but he or she is being stubborn in refusing to accept it. It may indicate physical or mental illness, but as I will say repeatedly: this is just for your information. It would be unethical to make a medical diagnosis or dispense medical advice.

WORK: Success comes to those who plant the best seeds and expect a fruitful harvest.
REVERSED: Times may be troubled; do not abandon hope but persevere.

LOVE: Someone looks at you with *starry* eyes; a new friendship may be just around the corner or an old one may be strengthened.
REVERSED: Love spurned, closure must be made.

MONEY: Protect your sources of income and watch unplanned expenses; a prosperous time is coming, but don't go through with incomplete plans or act on wild speculations.
REVERSED: Do not throw good money after bad; wait for the situation to improve.

FUTURE: Decide how best to spend your time. Focus on the goal; keep your eyes on the prize.
REVERSED: Prosperity is just around the corner, but which corner?

CARD #18—THE MOON

THE MOON.

THIS IS A CARD ABOUT
CYCLES, AND IT
DESCRIBES PEOPLE WHO
ARE INCLINED TO ACT ON
IMPULSE AND/OR THINK
INTUITIVELY. OLDER
BOOKS DESCRIBE THIS AS
A CARD ABOUT CHANGE
AND DECEPTION.

The Fool's Journey: *The Fool discovers the sensitive, intuitive side of his nature. Nine (8 +1 = 9) is the number of completion, arrival, integration, and realization—the transition between what once was and what now is.*

This is a difficult card to describe simply! Again, we see the repeated Tarot image of a path or character between two of something: here it is watchtowers. In the middle are a domesticated dog and a wild wolf—biologically the same creature, now in opposite polarities. A rugged path leads to higher levels of consciousness, suggested by the distant, lofty mountains. So, what is that crab/lobster/crawfish doing here? It is in an early stage of consciousness, rising out of the waters of the unconscious. The Querent must travel between the towers of good and evil to attain the goal of a higher state.

Another image that is repeated in Tarot is the multiphase representation of the moon. It is simultaneously full and in its first quarter. Some people read this as a time element. I usually ask my students to be aware of which phase the real moon is in when they conduct a reading. Depending on the phase of the (real) moon at the time, the events in their reading may take place by the next full moon or new moon, so it is easy to determine the length of time before these events can occur. The Moon can represent an area of unclear direction, a changeable future, or a time of frustration or anxiety for the Querent. It may be a time of intuitive dreaming, and is considered the card of psychics, poets, artists, and performers.

It is also a card about *cycles*—the beginning, end, or development of one—also possibly indicated by the phase of the (real) moon. Schedules, calendars, and clocks are important.

Older Tarot books emphasize the negative, historical aspects of the symbol of the Moon—particularly deception, changeability, and instability, utilizing the card as meaning unforeseen perils, bad luck for the Querent or an acquaintance, and a tendency toward negative thinking. The Moon has such a negative mythology that for thousands of years people believed that lunacy and countless other maladies were caused by *moonlight*.

REVERSED: If you understand the card to be negative when upright, then in reverse the Moon cancels out the negativity suggested, or the deceptive person will be revealed. It may suggest psychic powers are unfolding but underdeveloped; imagination may be affected by practical considerations. It may indicate a cycle of negativity is beginning or ending.

WORK: Keep track of how you spend your time: pace yourself according to your personal rhythm.
REVERSED: Try to get back in sync. Take no risks.

LOVE: When the (real) moon is full, anything can happen and does; don't expect to get much sleep.
REVERSED: Love may win, but not before it is almost destroyed by misunderstandings.

MONEY: Your financial stability waxes and wanes with the moon, but you will get by.
REVERSED: What appeared to be stable is showing its volatility. Look for ways to break this cycle.

FUTURE: Sleep on it; if it's not in the cards tonight, tomorrow is another day.
REVERSED: Remember, moonlight is reflected sunlight, so you may be better off waiting for the clarity of the sun to make your plans.

CARD #19—THE SUN

THE SUN.

THIS IS A CARD ABOUT
SUCCESS, ATTAINMENT,
INDEPENDENCE, AND
PERSONAL FREEDOM. IT
DESCRIBES PEOPLE WHO
ARE FREE SPIRITS AND
SHARE A CLOSE BOND
WITH NATURE—
GARDENERS AND SUN-
WORSHIPPERS.

The Fool's Journey: *The Fool obtains optimism and joy, knows contentment, and basks in the glow of success.*

A brilliant sun smiles down on a naked child riding a pony past a walled garden; the child has no worries and nothing to hide. It has a sense of innocence, yes, but a sense of accomplishment at a skill well learned or a conquest having been made. It can also indicate studies completed, good health, and success in business or the arts and sciences. Personally, I feel the Star and the Sun are interchangeable.

There are very few depictions of children in the Tarot, and many feel this card represents the Querent's child(ren), particularly a male child. It could indicate a happy marriage, possibly a long-awaited pregnancy and/or the birth of a child.*

*Once again—don't compromise your ethics. It is one thing to spout things off the top of your head as the spirit moves you to do so; it is another thing to tell someone to invest in the stock market or that their marriage will fail. It is also ill-advised to tell the Querent that she is pregnant or may be having a baby shortly. Don't set yourself up to be the "All-Knowing, All-Seeing Oracle of Truth." It will probably lead to trouble.

Can anything diminish the positive power of this card? If the Sun *appears* after a problem card, you can expect that the matter will be cleared up. If it appears *before* a problem card, you could remind the Querent that the Sun gives the power to overcome that problem. Even unbalanced news will have a feeling of contentment with the appearance of this card.

REVERSED: When reversed, picture in your mind that some thick clouds have come to cover the face of the Sun.

WORK: Rise, shine, and give God the Glory! Try out fresh, new ideas and new approaches to old problems that plague you.
REVERSED: This is not the day to bother your bosses with your personal agenda.

LOVE: Let love take you for a ride—let your hair down!
REVERSED: Suggests a broken engagement or a troubled marriage.

MONEY: The world is your oyster! Pull out your wallet and make that major purchase.
REVERSED: Bad stock for speculation, loss of a valued object.

FUTURE: The sky is the limit—fly by the seat of your pants! Don't worry about tomorrow—it will take care of itself.
REVERSED: Future plans clouded, failure at every turn.

CARD #20—JUDGMENT

JUDGEMENT.

THIS IS A CARD ABOUT
RENEWAL, AWAKENING,
AND DESTINY. IT
DESCRIBES PEOPLE WHO
ARE FACING A DECISION
ABOUT SOMETHING VERY
CRITICAL IN THEIR LIVES.
IT DENOTES A PERIOD
OF REFLECTION ON
PAST EVENTS.

The Fool's Journey: *Before his chance for redemption, a day of reckoning, The Fool receives an opportunity for assessment (or a time of testing).*

Another one of those cards whose image tends to put people off. A group of dead people rises naked from their coffins as the archangel Gabriel flies overhead blowing his trumpet, signaling that the time of reckoning is at hand. The first impression of most people is that they are being judged for their wrongdoings (a Western religious concept), will be found lacking, and will receive some kind of eternal, horrific punishment. Did the Fool get this close to enlightenment to be sent back to the torments of Hell? How does this card fit into the picture?

Is this judgment internal or external? Does it refer to the judgments received from others, such as a job performance review, or a legal judgment—or is it an *internal* judgment—how the Querents want to evaluate *themselves*? Enlightenment tends to mean *spiritual* enlightenment. What if the Querent is not a spiritual person?

Seeking the "beatific vision" would mean nothing to them. What are this judgment and its processes all about? Developing self-judgment through self-analysis is probably an individual's greatest challenge.

Perhaps the Querent needs to break away from conventional thinking and face life realistically, forging ahead and seeing what the future holds, free from previous thought patterns. Did a period of intense personal growth bring on a change of consciousness? The blasts from Gabriel's horn wake humans up from their earthly limitations.

This card can also indicate a job well done, renewed energies, improved health, and a sharper mind. The "testing" implied by the card should bring about success.

We have discussed this theory before: many Querents will find a judgment is made against them, despite their best efforts for success. We see this in many of the "change" cards; something extraneous overpowers them and they feel despair. What happens when a phone call or the actions of another appear to seal your fate or destiny? Is there nothing you can do? In Tarot—which Carl Jung described as being "of the moment"—nothing is written in stone. It is not the "bad news," but how you react or respond to that news that gives you control over your destiny.

> REVERSED: When this card is reversed, think of it as the dead being stuffed back into their coffins, or as Gabriel flying away without blowing his trumpet.

WORK: The clouds part and suddenly you can see where it all was leading or how it ends. The bottom line is suddenly revealed.
REVERSED: Fear of failure.

LOVE: Soon you will share a special experience with a dear friend.
REVERSED: Possible loss of love.

MONEY: Out of the blue, your material problems suddenly end or show improvement.
REVERSED: Failure of investments. Loss of income or savings.

FUTURE: Your struggles are coming to an end and "it" will be decided once and for all.
REVERSED: Fear of death, failure to find happiness, possible loss, and ill health.

CARD #21—THE WORLD

THE WORLD.

THIS IS A CARD ABOUT
TRIUMPH AND
UNPARALLELED SUCCESS,
REBIRTH, AND
REINCARNATION.

The Fool's Journey: *This card symbolizes completion, self-fulfillment, and enlightenment. With it the Fool acquires full knowledge and comprehension, happiness, and resolution.*

The final card of the Major Arcana! (Some consider the Fool [#0] to be card #22, which is considered the "master number" [4] that points to the manifestation of a higher level of understanding. I leave this up to you.) It is considered the "best" card in the deck to receive in a reading, particularly in the present or future. Even when it is reversed, a good reader will give encouragement instead of flatly declaring that things will "not be as good as when it is upright," an explanation I have always considered the ultimate cop-out. With this card comes the fulfillment of one's desires. The Querent will have the freedom to move ahead in undertakings, the ability to make others happier. A change of address or change of business/career may take place, possibly also increased travel. It can mean a great improvement in how others perceive your accomplishments and how those accomplishments will affect your upcoming goals. After all, success should not be considered an ending, but the start of even better things.

The cosmic dancer represents the final attainment of Man—the blending of the self, the conscious, unconscious, and the superconscious. As for the lion, the eagle, the bull, and the angel, we met these four symbols before in the Wheel of Fortune card, #10. They represent the four elements, the four fixed signs of the Zodiac, and also the four Gospels of the Bible. The wreath or circle symbolizes Nature on her unending course, and the ribbons also suggest the lemniscate, symbol of eternity. The World implies the final stage of enlightenment to which all the other cards in the Major Arcana have led.

> REVERSED: When this card is reversed, consider that the cosmic dancer has lost her footing and falls. However, like a true trouper, she will get up, brush herself off, and pick up her dance routine where she left off. This card may indicate a success yet to be won, a fear of change, a lack of vision, or the refusal to learn life's lessons as shown in the other cards.

WORK: The potential and the conditions are right to make just about anything happen.
REVERSED: Even if this job is wrong for you, use the experience it gives you to move forward.

LOVE: A fresh start, or everything seems fresh and new again.
REVERSED: Perhaps you are feeling "once burned—twice shy." You may be afraid to open yourself up to another for fear of being hurt.

MONEY: Be optimistic as conditions continually improve.
REVERSED: Make the necessary adjustments that can allow you to achieve your goals. In this position you are suffering from a lack of vision.

FUTURE: Give those ideas some space and time to grow and flourish. Expect nothing less than the best and it will come to you.
REVERSED: If at first you don't succeed . . .

THE MINOR ARCANA

T HE second section of the Tarot deck is known as the Minor Arcana (*arcane*—Latin for "secrets"), which encompasses the "pip" cards—cards numbered 1 to 10—and the Court cards. We will consider the Court cards separately in another section.

I affectionately refer to the Minor Arcana as "The Minors." This section of cards seems to correspond to the "modern" deck of regular playing cards, yet there are as many theories to dispute that fact as there are to support it. It is felt that the two sections of the deck were once separate entities that were joined at some point in time. Does it really matter if the modern deck evolved from Tarot or vice versa? Some people play a game called Tarrock or Tarrocchi that uses a Tarot deck but is not for divinatory purposes. Whatever its peculiar history, Tarot is what it is, and what historians say doesn't affect its validity.

"Older" Tarot decks such as the Marseilles Tarot have plain pip cards: that is, the Three of Cups pictures three cups, the Eight of Swords pictures eight swords. There are no symbols or scenes to jog your memory. This works well for the truly gifted or psychic; after all, everyone seems to have had a great-grandmother tucked away who "read" a deck of regular playing cards (this is known as cartomancy) without the benefit of special pictures. Thank the Powers That Be for Miss Pamela Coleman Smith! Under the direction of Arthur Waite, she created the 78 allegorical drawings that we now hold dear as the Rider-Waite deck! What a benefit for beginners!

I have chosen to teach the Minors in numerical order instead of in "suit" order. I feel that it might better help the student to know what is common to all cards of a particular number and then learn what makes each suit of the same number card slightly different. I will also start with the Aces (the Ones) and work through the Tens; I have always been truly annoyed with books that start with the tens and work backward. Likewise, I will put the Court cards in the last section in Page-Knight-Queen-King order so that when you have to find a card you can do so quickly, without aggravation.

My suggestion for you is to take the four cards being discussed and lay them out in front of you; in this way you might better see their similarities and differences.

THE ACES

The Aces (or Ones) are fairly consistent. A hand appearing out of a cloud holds the symbol for the suit. Because they depict the number "one," they indicate that a situation is about to begin or is in its early stages. Some people also feel that the Aces can indicate the season in which this beginning will start.

ACE of WANDS.

ACE of CUPS.

ACE of SWORDS.

ACE of PENTACLES.

THE ACE OF WANDS

ACE of WANDS.

THIS IS A CARD ABOUT OPPORTUNITIES THAT COME KNOCKING AT YOUR DOOR.

Go ahead—wave that magic wand—its power belongs to you.

Look at the thumb pointing up and think "thumbs-up," the symbol of approval for your business venture, a creative beginning, or a profitable journey. It may also suggest an inheritance, a new career, or even herald a birth in the family. Because there are leaves falling from the blossoming branch, some feel this represents the season of autumn.

REVERSED: Think "thumbs-down" on a particular project, suggesting the need to start over, rethink, or regroup.

WORK: Offers, promotions, school acceptances, or graduations.

LOVE: Favors are asked of you; a new relationship develops.

MONEY: Extra money in your pocket.

FUTURE: Send resumes, apply for new positions, and go to interviews.

THE ACE OF CUPS

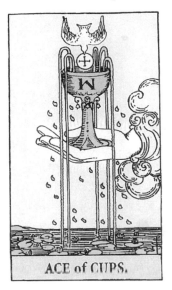

ACE of CUPS.

THIS IS A CARD ABOUT
OPPORTUNITIES THAT
COME OUT OF THE BLUE.

Drink from the cup and get in touch with your feelings.

Five streams of water (the life force?) pour over the edge of a goblet ("Your cup runneth over."). Whether it is love, joy, beauty, or health, it is a beginning of good things. It can also indicate a breakthrough in spiritual development (the dove with the wafer). The blossoming water lilies indicate the season of summer.

> REVERSED: When reversed, the waters have poured out and the cup is empty. Perhaps materialism, selfishness, or egotism has gotten in the way. Further development is necessary. There may be the fear of having to start over.

WORK: Deep friendships are being forged.

LOVE: Someone or something special is coming your way.

MONEY: Good fortune, positive cash flow.

FUTURE: "Drink in" the moment and enjoy it.

THE ACE OF SWORDS

ACE of SWORDS.

THIS IS A CARD ABOUT SUCCESS OR VICTORY (AFTER STRIFE) THAT SEEMINGLY COMES OUT OF NOWHERE.

Grab that sword and get ready for action.

We have been introduced to the two-edged Sword of Tarot in the Justice card, which can cut two ways. The crown has an olive branch of peace and the palm of victory (that droopy thing on the right) hanging from it. Love and hate—so closely related—can be construed from this card, as well as action, dynamics, being valiant, and using force, if necessary. The barren landscape below suggests the season of winter.

> REVERSED: When reversed, the two-edged sword indicates destructive behavior, or the use of too much force to gain an end. It may indicate that applying pressure will make a bad situation even worse. The embodiment of the upright meaning has now degenerated into dishonesty, lies, anger, and maybe deception.

WORK: You could be the hero of the hour if you would learn how to wield that sword.

LOVE: A strong attraction or an overpowering relationship.

MONEY: Increased buying power.

FUTURE: Carpe Diem! Seize the day! Nothing can stop you now!

THE ACE OF PENTACLES

THIS IS A CARD ABOUT
MONEY COMING TO YOU
OUT OF THIN AIR OR
FROM UNEXPECTED
SOURCES.

Take possession of that pentacle and count your riches.

Pentacles indicate materialism, material gain, and money, so this card is a good indicator of new ventures in finance. There is also happiness and appreciation of the good things in life. The well-tended garden indicates the season of spring.

> REVERSED: When reversed, the pentacle or coin falls from the hand and is lost. Great plans that were made may come to naught. Greed or miserliness. A loss of prosperity is unmistakable.

WORK: Financial backing, the beginning of prosperity.

LOVE: The material aspects of loving someone are involved; maybe a ring is bought.

MONEY: Money falls out of the skies—have your hands outstretched. It may be a good idea to play the lottery.

FUTURE: This is your lucky day! Enjoy it and rake in those chips.

THE TWOS

Twos indicate the involvement of another person; the situation cannot be handled or cannot develop while the Querent is alone. Twos indicate a period of *waiting* with more to be revealed later. Although Twos indicate stability, they also indicate duality, the pairing of opposites, and creativity not yet fulfilled.

THE TWO OF WANDS

THIS IS A CARD ABOUT
AMBITIONS AND
COOPERATIVE SHARING.

In this card a man stands patiently staring over the seas for "his ship to come in." Wands signify enterprise, energy, and growth. He has made his plans, sent his ship out, and is now waiting for the answer—will it come back full or empty? The seeker must exercise patience, for he cannot make the ship return any faster. Although he is well dressed, he probably had backers, and they, too, await the arrival of his ship. The interpretation is that he may have made the plans, but he could not have done it without help.

> REVERSED: When reversed, the Wands fall from his grasp and the world is turned upside down. Impatience is getting the better of him, and there is no movement towards a goal.

WORK: Partnerships, cooperative bargaining, or forming teams.

LOVE: A relationship based on something other than love. A marriage of convenience, or one partner is expecting the other to carry both of them.

MONEY: Backers are needed; someone puts up collateral.

FUTURE: Networking—seek those who can help you as you help them.

THE TWO OF CUPS

THIS IS A CARD ABOUT BONDING AND RELATION-SHIPS. ALTHOUGH IT BEARS A RESEMBLANCE TO THE LOVERS CARD (AND CAN BE READ INTERCHANGEABLY), IT ALSO INDICATES A BUSINESS PARTNERSHIP.

These two extreme sourpusses are supposed to be exchanging wedding vows! I think the artist was intending to show solemnity, but they look *so* unhappy! Here is an example of the balancing of forces, be it a new romance, a cooperative relationship, or a harmonious business partnership. (The lion indicates brute force, but his wings suggest a balance between spiritual and earthly love; the caduceus stands for life's positive and negative qualities.)

> REVERSED: When reversed, love turns to hate, trust to distrust, balance to disharmony. Divorce? Possibly, if you feel this card indicates marriage.

WORK: Partnerships; you receive an offer you can live with (or can't refuse).

LOVE: You find yourself making a commitment—be serious!

MONEY: Joint ventures; prepare to blend your money with someone else's.

FUTURE: Two heads are better than one, but get the agreement in writing.

THE TWO OF SWORDS

THIS IS A CARD ABOUT
THE BALANCE OF
FORCES. (ALSO KNOWN
AS THE "BETWEEN THE
ROCK AND THE HARD
PLACE" CARD.)

Put the swords down, take off the blindfold, and look around.

A blindfolded woman sits with her back to the sea (sometimes on a rock by a raging ocean) holding two swords. If she were to stand and try to walk, she could stumble and fall, and possibly cut or kill herself with the swords. *For the moment*, even though she is being battered on the one hand and in a precarious situation on the other, *she is balanced.* If she can maintain her balance until the situation changes, she will be better off enduring it than acting blindly, without knowing all the facts or possibilities. The card may also indicate a stalemate, or trouble ahead.

REVERSED: When reversed, think that the two swords have come together and decapitated the woman, although some interpret it as achieving the confidence to attain your goal. This will depend on the surrounding cards. The sliver of moon indicates deceptive, uncertain, or unreliable forces.

WORK: Points of view even each other out in a balance of power.

LOVE: Truce! More discussion and less action, please.

MONEY: Breaking even without gain.

FUTURE: Uphold your end of a compromise or bargain.

THE TWO OF PENTACLES

THIS IS A CARD ABOUT
BALANCING ASSETS
AND LIABILITIES.

A young man is juggling two proposals, trying to decide which one to accept. The sea of his emotions is rough, yet he seems able to maintain his balance in the midst of constant change. That is the secret of this card. (In one deck, the person is walking a tightrope and whistling to himself, suggesting that he knows he might be in a predicament but is trying to make the best of the situation.)

> REVERSED: When reversed, the Pentacles fall from his grasp or he falls off his tightrope. It may indicate that the Querent has "'too many irons in the fire," is disorganized, or receives a discouraging message that puts a damper on his or her ideas.

WORK: Keep a handle on expenses and the picture will improve.

LOVE: Conflicting views over money and money matters must get worked out.

MONEY: Balance that checkbook and keep your expenses in line with your income.

FUTURE: Maintain your balance! Focus on what you want all the way to the bottom line.

THE THREES

Threes usually indicate group activities or the involvement of more than one person. They can indicate delay, but suggest future success.

THE THREE OF WANDS

THIS IS A CARD ABOUT
DISTRIBUTION AND
PRODUCTIVITY.

The merchant from the Two of Wands now stands upon a mountaintop as ships sail past. His firm grip on his wand indicates that he is ready to receive the results of his planning—his ships have come in. Upright, this card indicates success in business affairs, trade, or commerce. Patience has paid off and the ships return full of cargo.

> REVERSED: When reversed, the ships are empty or have capsized; he loses his grip on his wands. It indicates the scattering of one's energies, careless mistakes, a strong competitor, or a caution against pride or arrogance.

WORK: Take a thorough inventory; strive for excellence.

LOVE: Learn how to package yourself—dress the part to attract or hold onto someone.

MONEY: Shop around and stretch your buying power.

FUTURE: Expect the best and you will receive it. Plan now for the best route to achieve your goals.

THE THREE OF CUPS

THIS IS A CARD ABOUT
GROUP ACTIVITY;
CARING AND SHARING
ARE INVOLVED.

Dancing maidens frolic with cups of wine amidst fruitful garlands and vines. A celebration of some sort—engagement, graduation, a wedding, or a baby shower—is being planned. It marks a time when we will be surrounded and supported by our friends. Arthur Waite also included "a healing in the offing" as an interpretation of this card, indicating that a long or grave illness is now over. Whatever it is—a party is involved. (It *could* be a wedding reception, but I feel the Four of Wands would say that better.)

REVERSED: When reversed the maidens trip and fall—perhaps, over-indulgence in food and drink? Pleasures turn to pain; gossip runs amok; ill health is a possibility. It also indicates a time to take command of yourself, to act more responsibly, and make new or different plans for the future.

WORK: A team effort concludes on a high note—an office party?

LOVE: You have the loving support of friends. (Don't laugh—it can also indicate an "I'm finally divorced" party!)

MONEY: Money is spent as a "thank you" gesture; an investment pays off. A mortgage burning, perhaps, or a barbecue?

FUTURE: Schmooze! Get to know others on a personal level. Interact with others more often.

THE THREE OF SWORDS

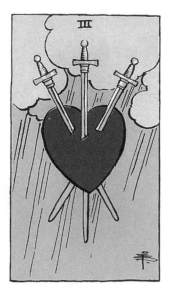

THIS IS A CARD ABOUT
DEEP HURT; IT RAINS ON
YOUR PARADE.

From dancing maidens we move on to storm clouds and a heart pierced with swords! This is a card you cannot soft-pedal; its image is unmistakable, and it usually gets a big reaction from the Querent! It says someone has stabbed you through the heart, someone close to you. It indicates separated lovers, family quarrels, social upheavals—definite unhappiness!

> REVERSED: When a "bad" card is reversed, some people figure that it has the opposite meaning from an upright card, and in this instance would indicate happiness and joy returning, but that is not usually the case. (The exception to this may be with the Fives, which are more positive when reversed—but more about this later.) Most books will tell you that "the intensity is less" than when it is in the upright position. So, how can you put a "favorable" spin on this card of deep sorrow? When the card is reversed, the swords fall out of the heart. Although the cause of the pain is gone and healing can start— the wound can and will heal—scar tissue will remain. Querents will be able to overcome this situation with time, and although they may never be able to completely erase the pain, they will learn to live with it, or view it differently, and endure. This is where the promise of future success lies.

WORK: Watch your back! Everybody's a critic, or holds a grudge.

LOVE: You are going to need to find a strong shoulder to cry on. A third party is indicated.

MONEY: Money is lost or a source dries up; bankruptcy, bad stock market investments. Remember: You are not an investment counselor, so don't tell the Querent the stock market will crash or which stocks to invest in or sell.

FUTURE: Develop a thick skin so that those arrows will glance off your back.

THE THREE OF PENTACLES

THIS IS A CARD ABOUT
ACHIEVING PROSPERITY;
IT REVEALS THE MASTER
BUILDER AT THE HEIGHT
OF HIS TALENTS.

Master builders are people at the height of their skills, mastery, abilities, pay scales, and success. They have experience behind them and material gains and success. (This contrasts with the Eight of Pentacles—the card of the apprentice. Some feel the placement of these cards should be reversed so that you start with the apprentice and then become the master builder as you go through the Pentacles, like The Fool on his journey.) It also indicates approval, congratulations, or the support of some undertaking. It is the card of the artist or craftsman.

> REVERSED: When reversed, the card indicates that you lack ambition, have mediocre job skills, and take the easy way out of most situations. Those expected rewards are slowed or delayed. You may have to be the first one to voice an idea to be able to get credit for it.

WORK: Apply the highest skills possible to the work at hand.

LOVE: Love triangle? Three is a crowd! (Be careful not to intimate that anyone is having an affair. It does not have to be a sexual thing.)

MONEY: A grant or an endowment could be in the offing.

FUTURE: Be able to demonstrate your abilities; you are the best one to show yourself off.

THE FOURS

Fours indicate fruition, or the manifestation of an idea, along with a foundation or "space" where things can grow.

THE FOUR OF WANDS

THIS IS A CARD ABOUT CELEBRATION.

Perhaps you have been asked to organize or attend a social event. Here is a card for people with public relations skills, restaurant workers, hotel staffs, event organizers, and clergy.

People dance and beckon you in to the party. This is generally the card for a wedding reception, but also a graduation or anniversary. In some decks, a couple dances on a square platform. The number four shows solidarity, prosperity, peace, happiness, abundance, or triumph.

REVERSED: This is such a good card that, even if reversed, it carries pretty much the same message. It indicates that one should learn to appreciate the beauty of the little things in life.

WORK: The career you have brings you in contact with a widely varied group of people.

LOVE: Some special occasion is indicated, so dress appropriately!

MONEY: Network—meet with people you wish to do business with.

FUTURE: Bread-and-butter notes, pleases, and thank-yous take you a long way.

THE FOUR OF CUPS

THIS IS A CARD ABOUT
CONTEMPLATION, THE
THOUGHT PROCESS, AND
OPPORTUNITY LOST.

A temporary period of inaction. Perhaps you are a bit confused and need time to sort things out in your own head.

A despondent young man sits beneath a tree with three cups in front of him. He is lost in thought: are the cups full or empty? Do they represent something he wants, wanted, or perhaps lost? Do they represent things he is refusing to accept? Is he paying attention to them at all? He is so lost in his own thoughts that he fails to notice a fourth cup materializing from nowhere. Could this fourth cup be the answer he seeks or needs? This card says pick up your head and look around! Don't let an opportunity pass you by because of neglect!

REVERSED: When reversed, the inactivity is now over; new relationships, goals, advancement, and ambition are possible.

WORK: Contemplating a career change? The proposition may be dangling right in your face.

LOVE: A temptation to stray even though a current relationship is satisfying.

MONEY: A decision to make with care, since the risk of capital is involved.

FUTURE: Proceed with caution! Know when and where to draw the line.

THE FOUR OF SWORDS

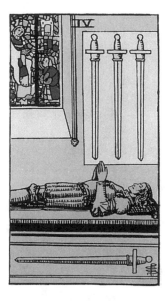

THIS IS A CARD ABOUT A
TIME FOR PREPARATION.

There is something you need to rest from or to get yourself psyched up for.

This is not a card of death! Many people get upset about the effigy on the coffin that is usually pictured on this card. Perhaps the Querent needs a time for retreat, or feels a sense of exile or temporary banishment. It may indicate a time of convalescence after illness. It may appear as a warning that the Querent is overextending himself and needs to pull back on the reins.

> REVERSED: When reversed, it speaks of renewed activities, "batteries recharged," good opportunities ahead, but a need to use discretion in one's dealings.

WORK: Everyone deserves to take a break, whether it's 10 minutes or a week's vacation.

LOVE: Chill out! Cool those jets! Stop tossing and turning and get some rest.

MONEY: Wait until tomorrow—tomorrow *is* just another day.

FUTURE: This is a time for waiting—tomorrow will come at its own pace.

THE FOUR OF PENTACLES

THIS IS A CARD ABOUT
POSSESSION AND
OWNERSHIP.

Is the Miser holding onto the coins because he simply does not want to share, or is he afraid of losing something forever?

The miserly character in this card tenaciously holds onto his money (or power). Although the number four expresses solidarity and strength of purpose, there are signs of being ungenerous here. However, the card's appearance can also indicate that a gift or inheritance will arrive shortly. Remember, too: the Querent may be afraid of losing something since it may be all that he has; greed may not be the only motivation.

REVERSED: When reversed, think that the Miser loses his grip and the coins fall from his grasp. A chance of loss, business obstacles, overextending financially, or being a spendthrift.

WORK: Acquire as much authority and territory as you can manage. Monetary compensation is low at this time.

LOVE: Someone is jealous of you, or being possessive.

MONEY: Excessive or compulsive behavior is going beyond "being prepared."

FUTURE: Keep a lid on your financial plans. Secure things of worth in a safe place.

THE FIVES

We now come to the Fives, and many things start to change. Whether you count from zero to nine or from one to ten, Fives are in the middle. Fives indicate change, challenge, and fluctuation. They may also indicate material prosperity but a spiritual poverty, being unbalanced or misunderstood. Here the negative sides of the suits are brought forward. As I see it, the Fives appear to be the only number where the upright cards seem consistently negative, and the reversed ones more positive. The Kabbalah sphere number 5 (Geburah) on the Tree of Life represents the breaking-down forces of nature, which are as necessary as the forces that build up.

Another new concept begins with the Five of Swords. Up to this point most of the cards we have dealt with have one central character who is easily identifiable as the Querent. Other characters are drawn on the same plane, such as in the Two of Cups. In the Five of Swords, however, there is a large, central character looking back at two figures walking away from him. Generally speaking, most readers see the central character—the largest one—as being the Querent or the Querent's actions. In this card there are the Defeated and the Victor. Which one is the Querent? Does the Querent feel defeated by someone or something and identify with the background figures while the central character signifies the oppressor? We will explore this concept of characters on different planes representing different people as we continue through the deck.

THE FIVE OF WANDS

THIS IS A CARD ABOUT
STIFF COMPETITION, FAIR
OR OTHERWISE.

Five young men are fighting with staves. From the look of things, there is no telling who the clear winner might be; after all, they are fighting each other as separate entities. If Wands deal with enterprise and glory, then these men are seeking a challenge, but the outcome is unclear.

If two of these men would band together and fight off the other three, they might win. This card is about strong competition in the Querent's field, or a quarrel with neighbors or in the home. It points to obstacles, possibly a lawsuit. This is a card about "spinning your wheels," for the more you try to accomplish, the less you will achieve because you are spreading yourself too thin, or working without a plan.

REVERSED: When reversed, think of the Wands as falling from the grip of the young men, and leaving them without a means to fight with each other. The opposite of strife is harmony in one's affairs, new opportunities, and hopes for a happy conclusion to unsettling events.

WORK: Bickering and feuding divide the ranks; management and labor do not see eye to eye.

LOVE: Real or imagined rivalry. May indicate your going to bat for someone else's honor.

MONEY: Competing needs and wants vie for your resources. You are struggling to make ends meet.

FUTURE: Preparing offensive and defensive strategies for the future cannot hurt.

THE FIVE OF CUPS

THIS IS A CARD ABOUT
DEEP SORROW OR
DESPAIR—THE LOSS OF
SOMETHING THAT
CANNOT BE RECOVERED.

A cloaked figure stands staring at three cups that have been knocked over and have spilled their contents. Whether by his doing or the actions of others, the deed has been done and there is no recovery. (No sense in crying over spilt milk.) Regardless of this, he can feel only despair over the loss. However, in his sorrow he has failed to notice the two cups untouched behind him—they are full (of promise). If he would only turn and see that opportunity is still available to him!

This card will usually strike a resonant chord in the Querent, particularly if it represents the loss of a loved one, or the breakup of a marriage. The emotions of the Cups, paired with the fluctuations of the number Five, speak of despair and agony over what is perceived as a great loss.

REVERSED: When reversed, while the loss cannot be recovered, the reversal of negative energies should bring a return of hope, the return of a friend or a loved one, but most importantly the courage needed to overcome the difficulties. A reader should find the best way to offer a positive outlook without giving the Querent false hope.

WORK: Success does not come as planned, if at all, or it comes at too great a price.

LOVE: A relationship gets permanently damaged. Saying "I'm sorry" is not enough.

MONEY: If there is a chance to recover, focus on what to do with your reserves.

FUTURE: Recover what you can and toss the rest. Do not look back.

THE FIVE OF SWORDS

THIS IS A CARD ABOUT
SELF-DEFENSE. ARE YOU
THE CONQUEROR OR THE
CONQUERED?

The thrill of victory is experienced by one and the agony of defeat by another.

A man with a most *un*sportsmanlike smile gloats over his victory in getting his opponents' swords, while they retreat unhappily in the distance. Was this a fair fight, or was trickery involved? Did he win justly, or just for the sake of winning? Cowardice, cruelty, malice—all these things can be seen in his defiant stance. Maybe he just stole them outright? This is not the easiest card to have, so study the surrounding cards to accurately describe the outcome.

REVERSED: When reversed, I wouldn't exactly say the situation improves, but perhaps the defeat will not be as great, or as long lasting; the perpetrator will realize it was an empty victory. The card still indicates that there are rumors and gossip about, so be careful in dealings with others.

WORK: A personality clash is involved. You may have to prove not only your point, but also yourself in the process.

LOVE: A triangle breaks up. One person emerges the victor out of a set of contenders.

MONEY: Others may be losing their shirts; don't lose yours. However, their loss may become your gain—if you survive.

FUTURE: Bluffing your way through may not work this time; you will be required to take action and defend your position.

THE FIVE OF PENTACLES

THIS IS A CARD ABOUT
THE LACK OF SUPPORT,
A BREAKDOWN OF
BELIEF SYSTEMS, OR
THE EFFECTS OF
BAD CHOICES.

Two street people in a blinding snowstorm struggle past the warm, lighted refuge of a church. Perhaps they have "failed to see the light." Or perhaps their old system of beliefs no longer works for them. Perhaps they have made a series of poor choices. This card is about feeling destitute, lonely, abandoned, or being unemployed. It may even indicate poor or failing health. Small wonder that it is referred to as "the dark night of the soul" card. It says you feel as though you have been left out in the cold.

REVERSED: When reversed, as in the rest of the Fives, the situation may improve, but it will not be completely reversed or revert back to normal. It may represent new employment, but that may be only temporary. The Querent should receive new encouragement, as bad luck seems to reverse, but should be cautioned that the cause of the situation might still be lingering. It does indicate improved health, but not immediately. Perhaps, if there was a spiritual lack, the Querent will be moving on to a new level of understanding, or learning a lesson in compassion.

WORK: The ends are no longer meeting, and desperate measures may result.

LOVE: Tough it out. You have no one but each other to rely on at this time (if you see the people in the card as a couple).

MONEY: The prospects of getting through this have less to do with financial resources than personal ones.

FUTURE: Bolster your courage and get through the night. You have few options but to depend on others, and on your own wits.

A note about artistic styles and interpretation: European-style decks are broken into "Continental" and "English" decks. One difference is clearly noted in the Five of Pentacles card. English decks, like the Rider-Waite, show the sickly poor freezing outside a well-lit, warm church, warning of the painful outcome of bad choices or feeling abandoned. In Continental decks (such as the Tarot of the Stars, an Italian deck), a young couple sits in a garden bower. Holding hands and appearing very friendly, their facial expressions and body language indicate that what they are saying and what they want are two different things. Both of them are jockeying for the best advantage and it is unclear who is pursuing whom at the moment.

In the Continental deck it is a card about mergers and opportunities, and the emotional exhilaration that could sidetrack one from being practical about the details—a far cry from being frozen in a blinding snowstorm! Depending on which type of deck you use, you'll need to learn to shift your way of thinking. Although card interpretation can be universal, artistic variations can change the meaning of the card, sometimes in unexpected ways.

THE SIXES

The Sixes indicate adjustments in thoughts, attitudes, or conditions. They can also represent the ability to transcend difficulties. Sixes stand for balance and equilibrium.

THE SIX OF WANDS

THIS IS A CARD ABOUT
TRIUMPH AND VICTORY.

A man on horseback wearing the laurels of victory is honored with some type of parade celebrating his achievement or leadership qualities. This is a card of good news, victory achieved, success from hard labors. It can also indicate the joyful conclusion of these matters.

> REVERSED: When reversed, the rewards are delayed. Something may be postponed, but that may be for the best, even if that cannot be seen at present. It may indicate the news of someone else's victory, or a celebration tainted by some bad news.

WORK: You can expect triumph in an upcoming competition or the landing of a desired position.

LOVE: You may be enamored of a public figure, such as a rock star, movie star, or politician. Perhaps you will see someone you care about receive an award.

MONEY: Strong performance on the job improves your cash flow; blow your horn a bit.

FUTURE: Once you access the purpose of your mission—attack!

THE SIX OF CUPS

THIS IS A CARD ABOUT
NOSTALGIA AND
SENTIMENTAL VALUES.

A young boy presents a bouquet of flowers to a younger companion. On some decks it looks as if they are in a garden, but others show the wall as a bridge, over which the young man will pass into adolescence, leaving the things of childhood behind. This card denotes a connection or reconnection to something in the past—either meeting an old acquaintance, pleasant memories of the past, a message from someone you've lost contact with, or possibly an inheritance. It may indicate new opportunities or moving to new surroundings. It is okay to live *with* the past, but don't live *in* the past. As Thomas Wolfe wrote: "You can't go home again." I remember this card appearing in the reading of a man who was seeking employment opportunities, and I said, "In your past *is* your future." It turned out he had once worked as a carpenter, and was undecided about taking a new job with a construction company. He went out and applied for the construction job, and got it.

REVERSED: When reversed, you have a disappointment. Perhaps you are clinging to outworn manners or thinking, or are afraid to face the present. Perhaps the memory of something was better than the reality of it. It may be an indication to cut the ties of the past. Or it could mean disappointment over an inheritance.

WORK: Get to know your coworkers to understand where they are coming from.

LOVE: An old fire may be rekindled, but with new tinder. You hear from old friends.

MONEY: A little goes a long way; it's the thought, not the cost, that counts.

FUTURE: Take a lesson from the past. Times do change even if people don't.

THE SIX OF SWORDS

THIS IS A CARD ABOUT A
FLIGHT TO SAFETY, BY
RUNNING AWAY EITHER
FROM SOMETHING OR
TOWARD SOMETHING.

Much has been made of this card—does it show a family, dejected and fleeing a disaster, either natural, or self-made? Is the man a ferryman helping a woman and child flee from an abusive spouse? Can it indicate mental illness—a flight from reality?

When a situation becomes intolerable, and you feel too weak or have been weakened by the situation, sometimes running is the best option. On the right the waters are turbulent, but the boat is moving into calmer waters as it approaches land. This card may not be as somber as it appears—it may merely indicate a journey over water.

REVERSED: The journey is delayed or there is no immediate way out of the difficulties. No matter how difficult the situation, the "flight" part may be impossible or contraindicated at the moment.

WORK: A job may be abandoned for one with more promise.

LOVE: May indicate either the end of loving, or that the couple will share a journey, if they are able to leave the past behind.

MONEY: Moving or relocating. Be prepared to bail out quickly.

FUTURE: Leave the situation fast and far behind you.

THE SIX OF PENTACLES

THIS IS A CARD ABOUT
GENEROSITY, EITHER
FINANCIAL OR
SPIRITUAL GIVING.

Are you the rich man or one of the beggars? Here is another one of those cards with figures on two planes. A man with scales shares gold in balanced judgment. If people are looking to you for help and encouragement—don't let one hand know what the other is doing and give lovingly with no strings attached. This card could indicate that the Querent will receive what is rightfully his—an inheritance, philanthropy, gifts, perhaps unemployment benefits, or worker's compensation. If the Querent is prone to charitable giving, the adage about "Bread thrown on the waters of Life" will return threefold, and his charity will benefit himself as well.

REVERSED: When reversed, it looks as though the coins are going from the poor man's hands to the rich one—a sign of bribery, perhaps, or dirty dealings in high places. It definitely indicates unfairness in business or in the distribution of an estate. Perhaps investments have lost their value, or there is miserliness or jealousy. It may indicate that you have something to learn from people who are less fortunate than you are.

WORK: Could indicate a raise is coming or bonuses are being handed out.

LOVE: Could deal with a child's allowance, borrowing the car, or lending some help to a relative.

MONEY: You may have more than enough to meet your own expenses, so you might consider making donations to a charitable organization.

FUTURE: If people come for advice, be sure to give them your two cents' worth. Can indicate a small sum of money coming when you need it most.

THE SEVENS

Sevens denote a period of introspection or solitude. They deal with wisdom, completeness, and perfection, and relate to the development of the soul.

THE SEVEN OF WANDS

THIS IS A CARD ABOUT
DEFENDING YOURSELF.

You may need to protect your turf, support your views, or muster people to your battle cry.

A young man faces an onslaught from six unseen foes. Although he is outnumbered, he is defiant—maybe even confident. Notice that he is on top of a hill, so even if all his opponents were to charge him, they would be more likely to lose their footing than would he. This gives him the advantage, even though victory depends on his energy and courage. This card deals with the ability to hold one's own against competition and adversaries.

REVERSED: When reversed, think that all have lost their grip on their wands; without weapons they cannot fight. This indicates that the threat may pass you by, but continue to be wary and don't let others take advantage of you. It is also a caution against indecision.

WORK: Take the high ground and fight if necessary.

LOVE: Put up a good line of defense against unwanted advances.

MONEY: Someone is trying to bully you into buying or selling.

FUTURE: Define your position and defend it; rally the support of others if need be.

THE SEVEN OF CUPS

THIS IS A CARD ABOUT
DREAMING.

Your head is full of hopes and desires.

Bizarre and fantastic visions rise from seven cups floating in front of a man. He does not know which to choose! Some are real opportunities; some are possibilities; some are merely wishful thinking.

His attention is scattered as he tries to decide where to look next. This card deals with being unfocused or having an overactive imagination. There is nothing wrong with dreams; after all, without dreams we would have nothing to strive for. However, indulging in endless dreaming will get you nowhere. The trick is to decide what is practical, what has possibilities, and what is a waste of time. Make a choice! Stop dreaming and start doing!

For the curious: The castle could indicate a new home or business, the jewels a desire for wealth. The wreath with the skull stands for victory, the dragon for temptation, the serpent for jealousy. The floating head could represent either the ideal woman or the idealized self, and the draped figure, the Querent's own divinity waiting to be uncovered.

REVERSED: When reversed, a choice has been made, and a definite plan of action has been drawn up. It shows a good use of determination and will. Any small successes should be followed up.

WORK: The future may seem rosy, but there are unseen strings attached. Choose carefully.

LOVE: A relationship holds great promise (or may provide you with good connections).

MONEY: A bright future is indicated, but don't spend your expected earnings yet.

FUTURE: You have the chance to impress someone; use your most convincing arguments.

THE SEVEN OF SWORDS

THIS IS A CARD ABOUT ESCAPING UNDETECTED.

This card can be either positive or negative depending on the surrounding cards.

A man tiptoes away (or climbs over a wall) from a military encampment carrying swords he has obviously stolen from the tents behind him. The group of soldiers (bottom left in the Rider-Waite deck) is oblivious to what has happened. The traditional interpretation for this card is theft (from the Querent). It deals with unreliability, vicious gossip, two-faced people, betrayal, and *also* the flight from a dishonorable act. The card usually serves as a warning about the actions of others, but it may implicate the Querent.

> REVERSED: When reversed, a theft is thwarted, or a thief returns what has been taken. An apology may be forthcoming, or a person who is keeping a secret from you will reveal the deception.

WORK: Secrets are being leaked. Private files are being read. Or maybe you just want to leave work early!

LOVE: Someone is not telling you everything you need to know.

MONEY: A con job may be in the works; small amounts of money seem to disappear.

FUTURE: If you get caught, you'd better find a good excuse—and fast.

Some Alternative Views of the Seven of Swords

This card functions on several different levels, some of which I'm sure Waite never foresaw.

Once again, we have figures on different planes: the large central figure of the thief and the smaller figures (in most decks) of the soldiers themselves. Are you the man with the swords or the men in the tents? Are you being warned of a theft that is about to happen to you, or are you about to commit a crime, or have you already committed one? This could include everything from grand theft auto to white-collar crime—"downsized" people who remove the contents of their cubicle and desk whether the objects belong to them or not.

Then again, the Querent might be *neither*—but merely an observer of the actions in this card. Or the Querent might be a third party to illegal happenings: maybe he or she is allowing a bad situation to exist; turning a deaf ear or blind eye to a situation, thinking that is preferable to "getting involved"; or he or she might be involved as the "lookout."

On a personal level, I have seen this card come up many times for people who are thinking of changing jobs. They are actively looking for a new situation. Here, the "theft" is not the contents of their desks, but something intangible—job skills or job training—that they are taking with them.

THE SEVEN OF PENTACLES

THIS CARD IS ABOUT
PROFIT ON AN
INVESTMENT.

A farmer rests from the cultivation of his crops. He has labored hard, but the harvest is still in the future, and its outcome is still unknown. Some crops will mature quickly; some will take a longer time; but some may *never* mature or may wither on the vine. Right now nothing can be done except to have patience and wait for the time to be ripe. It is a period of pause or reevaluation in the developmental process.

REVERSED: When reversed, it means you have grown impatient or anxious. Possibly, investments have proved unprofitable or there has been little gain after much work.

WORK: It looks as though your hard work is about to pay off.

LOVE: You are off to a good start, although there is much room for future growth.

MONEY: Think about investing or reinvesting you earnings, or consider taking out stock options. (Remember—you are not a market analyst. Be careful what you suggest to the Querent.)

FUTURE: You cannot rush the future, so sit back and relax for the moment.

THE EIGHTS

Eight indicates a positive change of mind or status because the beneficial qualities of the number eight (2 times 4, the number of manifestation) are rarely diluted. Eight is the number of justice, judgment, material progress, and *health*.

THE EIGHT OF WANDS

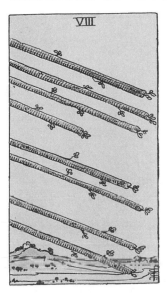

THIS IS A CARD ABOUT
PROJECTS, GOALS,
TARGETS—AND
FORWARD MOTION.

Eight wands are flying through the air, although their forward movement is lessening and their trajectory seems to be carrying them back to earth. They can represent new ideas, goals, careers, resumés, projects in the works, love letters, e-mails; also a journey by air or love of open spaces, including gardening or field sports. If you were to take a handful of arrows and shoot them at a single target, some would hit the mark, and some would miss entirely.

REVERSED: When reversed, it is time to slow down and reorganize. Stand back and observe rather than jump in blindly or try to force your hand. This card may indicate jealousy, violence, quarrels, and disputes; possibly an awaited message does not arrive, or the answer is not what was anticipated.

WORK: Keep sight of what brought you to this job in the first place; launch long-term projects.

LOVE: Two people sharing a common path are heading for the same goals together.

MONEY: A check is in the mail; time payments may be indicated.

FUTURE: Get their attention by firing off a barrage of ideas, proposals, or resumés.

THE EIGHT OF CUPS

THIS IS A CARD ABOUT
RETIRING OR
RETREATING.

Someone wants to chuck it all, run away, and start all over again. A feeling of disappointment has created a desire for change.

A man walks away from eight cups he has carefully stacked. Are they empty, and is he walking away disconsolate, rejecting the company of people? Are they full, but is he, like the unfulfilled prince, seeking something better? Perhaps he is rejecting materialism in hopes of seeking and finding something higher, or he has had a disappointment in love. Whatever it is, he walks towards the barren mountains unsure of his fate, but determined to search for it. It also could represent someone whose company "downsized" and who is looking for ways to come to grips with the situation. In its extremes it may indicate mental illness—a withdrawal from society.

Once again, the moon is pictured in both its full and waning quarter. It can be a time indicator, depending on the position of the actual moon at the time of the reading. For example, there is a week's difference between the full moon and the last quarter. If your reading takes place at the dark of the moon, the events indicated could happen in as soon as two weeks. If you happen to be within the final quarter, the events could be happening by the next full moon, or within three weeks.

REVERSED: When reversed, it can indicate that the Querent is seeking earthly pleasure instead of spiritual enlightenment, but mostly it can indicate a renewed interest in someone he or she was once estranged from. It may also indicate that the Querent has found the answer that was sought, and is now returning from the quest.

WORK: Maybe it is time to change direction, since a corporate relationship may have gone as far as it can go.

LOVE: Someone needs to be cut some slack and allowed to work something out alone. Offer your support but allow that person some space.

MONEY: Walking or getting away right now may be the best thing to do.

FUTURE: Expand your horizons, even if you just take an afternoon's drive. A change of scenery can work wonders.

THE EIGHT OF SWORDS

THIS IS A CARD ABOUT
FEELING TRAPPED
OR BEING CAPTURED,
PHYSICALLY OR
MENTALLY.

A bound and blindfolded woman stands on unsure ground while the eight swords around her bear an uncanny resemblance to prison bars (one interpretation is someone in prison). She cannot see what is ahead of her—she could easily trip and fall, possibly against the swords, and get mortally wounded. The Querent feels censure, has restricted action through personal indecision, or is at the mercy of someone or something. Perhaps illness has robbed him or her of the strength to fight back. Unlike the woman in the Two of Swords, who knows inaction is the best choice for *her*, this woman has no choice.

> REVERSED: When reversed, the bonds and blindfold slip off and new beginnings become possible. This card indicates a relaxation after fear, and a freedom from restriction. It may indicate that someone in prison will soon be released.

WORK: Your hands are tied; the chances of making progress are minimal at best.

LOVE: Someone seeks to control you, or doesn't meet your needs.

MONEY: Money troubles abound. Make a last-ditch effort, but don't be careless.

FUTURE: Plan your escape route, but do not act on it at present. Things may appear desperate, but don't give up!

THE EIGHT OF PENTACLES

THIS IS A CARD ABOUT WAGES, SKILL DEVELOPMENT, OR A LEARNING EXPERIENCE IN GENERAL.

The apprentice chisels out his umpteenth pentacle in an attempt to learn his trade, since developing his skills will lead to employment or commissions to come. (Compare this with the Three of Pentacles, the Master Builder.) This card can literally indicate continuing education classes, or a change of career that requires learning or relearning on or outside the job. It often appears for someone with an interest in the arts. Indicates financial gain but in small amounts.

REVERSED: When reversed, the apprentice is off his workbench, walking around. This can mean the Querent dislikes hard work or work in general. Might also indicate a wrong use or waste of skills in the present job. It can also represent a slowdown in production or a work strike.

WORK: Achieving quality will result in increased earnings.

LOVE: A few rough edges need work, but this arrangement handled correctly can pay back handsomely.

MONEY: Money or time invested will put money back in your pocket

FUTURE: Take pride and put your best foot forward. Then negotiate for more money!

THE NINES

Nines indicate that situations or events are nearing completion or have just been completed, and another plateau waits.

THE NINE OF WANDS

THIS IS A CARD ABOUT
YOUR DUTY TO YOURSELF
OR OTHERS; YOU ARE
EXPECTED TO TAKE YOUR
RESPONSIBILITIES
SERIOUSLY.

A wounded man is standing guard in front of a fortress-like structure. He is leaning on his wand for support, but is wary of the area around him. The bandage on his head indicates that he has fought before, and he is ready to fight again for what is right. This is a card about being prepared, personal victory, or conserving your strength if you believe more fighting must be done.

It can indicate a return to health, but also a tendency to be obstinate. This man is so concerned for the welfare of others (or maybe himself) that he is standing guard in self-sacrifice.

REVERSED: When reversed, it is time to regroup. You need to rest and recuperate and let someone else stand guard. Can also indicate a lack of preparation, or a weakness of character. It bodes ill health, possible mental ill health ("They're out to get me!").

WORK: Keep up your guard. You are being tested, but passing the test is not as important as not failing it.

LOVE: Is jealousy involved? Someone wants to test your loyalty.

MONEY: Protect your sources of income; meet your obligations.

FUTURE: You can't trust everyone or be too careful.

THE NINE OF CUPS

THIS IS A CARD ABOUT
SATISFACTION AND
CONTENTMENT.
(KNOWN AS THE "PARTY
HEARTY" CARD.)

A robust, well-dressed man sits in front of nine cups that represent his material success. He lacks for nothing; his future well-being seems assured. Some readers ask the Querent to make a wish before their reading; and if this card appears, the Querent is certain to get his wish. (It is also known as the "wish card.") It says, "Tomorrow we may die, but we're gonna have one hell of a party tonight!"

> REVERSED: When reversed it can represent a lack of resources or money, and also a tendency toward overindulgence in food or drink. There may be some illness involved, but it is not of a lasting nature. The wish will not be fulfilled. Of course, if the card *doesn't* come up, the wish will not come true, either.

WORK: Things are working out for you and/or you may be honored in some way.

LOVE: The satisfaction is mutual—someone makes you feel good.

MONEY: You are well clothed and fed; just sit back and enjoy it.

FUTURE: Hang on to a good thing—why tamper with a winning streak?

THE NINE OF SWORDS

THIS IS A CARD ABOUT
THE PAIN OF MENTAL
ANGUISH.

A sleeper having a bad dream or reliving a haunting memory sits bolt upright in bed, crying in anguish, frozen in terror. This card indicates misery, suffering, desolation, illness (of the Querent or someone he or she knows), or receiving bad news. It can also be anguish over *another's* cruelty, dishonesty, or even slander.

REVERSED: When reversed, the swords are dispelled and the sleeper lies back down to rest. Good news about a loved one is received. Time will bring healing. Tomorrow is another day, and its light can dispel the ghosts of the night. (Here is another card that is more positive in a reversed placement.)

WORK: A nagging thought troubles you; perhaps it is not too late to do something about it.

LOVE: Realization comes too late to undo any damage. If someone wants to make amends, hear them out.

MONEY: The financial damage may not be as extensive as you thought, but the loss cannot be recovered.

FUTURE: You keep running scripts in your head to come up with a revised version of what you said. Try to say the right thing the next time.

THE NINE OF PENTACLES

THIS IS A CARD ABOUT
THE VALUE OF MONEY.

Purchases are made to improve your environment or enrich your surroundings.

A richly dressed woman wanders through her beautiful garden; she carries a hooded bird of prey on a gloved hand. In the background a manor house looms. This card often appears in the layout of mature women who are widowed or single, independent, and well-off. She has the money (and staff) to maintain the house and garden; she has leisure time enough to train a falcon to hunt.

This is a card about material well-being, a solitary enjoyment of the good things in life. It can also indicate those with an intense interest in gardening or a passion for their home as their castle. They may do things to "make the Jones's jealous," but they know the value of a dollar. The card may indicate a possible inheritance.

REVERSED: When reversed there is a fear of loss—generally of material things that took hard work to acquire. There could also be a loss of security, possibly a theft, or a loss of friendship. Beware of legal entanglements.

WORK: You have worked hard and now it is time to do something nice for yourself.

LOVE: Dress up! Dress sharp! Those little things help keep love alive.

MONEY: An emphasis on the external, putting money into things that show.

FUTURE: You know where your interests lie—gather strength from the material world around you and the people you attract or are attracted to.

The Downside of the Nine of Pentacles

There are a couple of aspects to this card that do not get mentioned often, but they're still there, even when the cards are upright.

In one artist's vision of the garden, there is a large, beautiful, but securely locked iron gate. Is it there to keep the riffraff out, or does it keep the people locked within, prisoners of their own fears? They have acquired all these things, but now are afraid that everyone will try to steal from them ("They're rich—they'll never notice" or "We're rich—people will try to take our wealth").

In another deck, the woman is pictured inside the manor house looking out at the gardens and world around her. The grate over the window has a bar-like or cage-like quality to it. Is she being kept against her will, surrounded by beautiful things but feeling empty or trapped inside? Or is she *not* a widow at all but someone's live-in mistress? After all, this woman has no visible means of support, nor does she partake in the upkeep of the manor. Think about it.

THE TENS

The Tens can be read the same way as the Aces (10: 1 + 0 = 1); however, Tens signify the cyclical re-beginning, and a time when you must come to terms with something you may have avoided in the past. The Tens show the ultimate quintessence of each suit. The Cups and Pentacles show the heights of bliss; the Swords and Wands show the depths of tribulation.

THE TEN OF WANDS

THIS IS A CARD ABOUT
THE BURDENS WE BEAR.

A man carrying a heavy burden of wands plods along a road, straining, but hoping he'll reach the city in the distance before he drops one. Did someone else dump this burden on him, or did he take it on himself, not expecting it to be so heavy? Perhaps this is the card of the workaholic or overachiever, always taking on more and more because he doesn't know anything else. One false move and there will be ruin and disruption. Will one more straw break the camel's back?

> REVERSED: When reversed, the wands fall from the man's arms and there are three possible meanings: 1) the burden has been dropped and all is lost; 2) the burden has been lifted; or 3) the burden has been shifted onto someone else. This meaning will probably be indicated by the surrounding cards.

WORK: Feeling overburdened or stretched too far, you've been putting in a lot of hours.

LOVE: Family obligations get you down; try and get away for a while—and stop feeling guilty.

MONEY: You find yourself working *twice* as much to get half as far.

FUTURE: *Get help!* The amount of energy needed exceeds your limits.

THE TEN OF CUPS

THIS IS A CARD OF STEREOTYPICAL HAPPY ENDINGS; IT'S AS GOOD AS IT GETS.

The Ten of Cups and the Ten of Pentacles are almost interchangeable, but they do have a few differences. In this card a young couple sees the rainbow of joy and promise appear over their modest home, while their children dance for joy. Here are lasting happiness, true friendships, and a happy home life inspired from above. A special moment is being shared.

> REVERSED: A family quarrel, loss of friendships, or a chance of betrayal. A desire for happiness that hasn't completely arrived yet. Wantonness, waste, debauchery.

WORK: Work can wait! Your family should come first—they can't lay you off!

LOVE: A storybook relationship lives up to your mutual expectations.

MONEY: And what is the purpose of money? Enjoy it while you can.

FUTURE: Spend quality time together with a loved one someplace without distractions.

THE TEN OF SWORDS

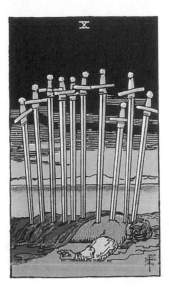

THIS IS A CARD ABOUT
BETRAYAL AND DEFEAT—
BUT NOT DEATH.

Another card whose image cannot be sidestepped: A man lies face down in a pool of his own blood stabbed through with ten swords. Whoever was out to get you got you good—or did you do this to *yourself*? Are you digging yourself an early grave? Swords symbolize the ultimate of what strife, hatred, and aggression can do. Indicates ill health, sudden misfortune, and defeat in a battle or lawsuit.

> REVERSED: When reversed, the swords fall out. The wounds can heal, and although the scar tissue of hurt will remain, even that can be borne with help. The card indicates a steady improvement in health, and that any losses are now in the *past*. New horizons and positive cycles can begin.

WORK: Watch your back and keep your nose clean!

LOVE: Not only is this relationship over, but it ends on a sour note.

MONEY: Financial ruin from shady business dealings.

FUTURE: Trust no one any farther than you can throw them. Do not take any knowing risks.

THE TEN OF PENTACLES

THIS IS A CARD ABOUT
MATERIAL WEALTH
AND MEANS.

A multigenerational family gathers near an archway containing their family coat of arms. This happy family differs from the one pictured in the Ten of Cups, which dealt with emotional happiness. This family has acquired wealth, honor, prestige, and property. The card indicates a large inheritance and financial stability. Think old money and ivy-covered walls.

> REVERSED: When reversed, there is a chance of family misfortune or dishonor, family disharmony. The card cautions against getting involved in a poor financial risk. There may be problems with a will or pension.

WORK: Great success. Perhaps you reap the profits of a family-run enterprise.

LOVE: A high-maintenance love affair, but worth it.

MONEY: You want it? You've got it!

FUTURE: Acquire! Pay cash for everything and live happily ever after.

THE COURT CARDS

ALTHOUGH the Court cards are a continuing part of the four suits, I have separated them into their own section for good reason. The Court cards—Pages, Knights, Queens, and Kings (also called the Princess, Prince, Girl, Boy, Woman, or Man) are some of the most enigmatic cards. Many readers have sweated through them and found a "system" that works for them, and no two readers ever seem to have the same interpretation for any two cards.

The Court cards work on many levels—sometimes simultaneously! They take a little deciphering. They could be bad news, a positive change, or the office gossip in the next cubicle. Perhaps they are a reflection of the Querent's personality.

We are going to start with the lowly Page and work our way through to the Kings. Many people assign a specific gender, age, and coloring to the Court cards in an attempt to make them more usable. Some readers do this to create a "Significator" card, which is used to represent the Querent, putting it in the center of the table and placing the first card over it (see page 16). To most of us, the Court cards look androgynous, even the Queens and Kings. Remember that we all have our masculine/feminine sides and qualities, and a King could just as easily represent a woman's masculine side.

THE PAGES

Pages may represent both boys and girls from a young age up until adolescence. The Page can represent the Querent or someone the Querent knows, but this character is usually the message (or the messenger) bringing some news or information to the Querent. The different Pages bring different types of messages. In my readings, when a Page is turned over, I usually finish laying out all the necessary cards for the spread, and then flip the top card off the pack onto the Page as a clarifying card, to find out what the message is about. (Note: You can clarify *any* card in a reading using this method, but wait until you have finished laying out the spread. Then go back and flip the top card off the pack.)

Some people will automatically tell you that a Page—a young person suddenly coming into your life—represents the birth of a child, but don't get carried away with this.

REVERSED: A reversed Page (any Page) can indicate that no news is forthcoming or that it is delayed, misinformation is given, or the message is not what was expected.

PAGES

PAGE of WANDS.

PAGE of CUPS.

PAGE of SWORDS.

PAGE of PENTACLES.

THE PAGE OF WANDS

PAGE of WANDS.

THIS IS A CARD
ABOUT OFFICIAL
COMMUNICATIONS.

Someone may have something important to tell you. More likely you will receive news that relates to your job, studies, or career.

The Page of Wands stands poised like the town crier, ready to bang the end of his wand against the ground to get your attention. The news he brings is important indeed! It could be a letter, fax, phone call, e-mail, or plain conversation.

UPRIGHT PERSONALITY

Good communicator, strong and dynamic person who is likely to be a good friend and who will always tell it like it is. Capable of great enthusiasm, courage, and inner beauty.

Example: A younger person who is eager to experience work or social activities, loves to be in the spotlight, possibly on the debating team.

MESSAGE / NEWS

The message may come from a younger person or friend and is very positive.

REVERSED PERSONALITY

A superficial, theatrical, overzealous, or image-conscious person. *Example:* A person who feels unloved and is out to get attention. *Be on guard!* This is the bearer of false or misleading information and not someone who can be trusted.

MESSAGE / NEWS REVERSED

Upsetting or unfavorable news or delays in travel plans. Generally speaking, regardless of which Page appears, a reversed Page indicates delays; the messenger is not able to deliver the news correctly, or the message is correct but not what the Querent wants to hear.

WORK: A job in communications may be involved or you may find employment through the want ads or the grapevine.

LOVE: You or your partner has been disclosing too many details of your love life. A favorable review is one thing—but you are revealing too much!

MONEY: You will be reimbursed or hear about your salary or benefits. A loan you applied for should be given a green light.

FUTURE: The situation requires you to get information around quickly, so hit that e-communication to get the word out!

THE PAGE OF CUPS

PAGE of CUPS.

THIS IS A CARD ABOUT
GREETINGS AND
SALUTATIONS.

A sloppy or mushy love letter, greeting card, or thank-you note. A wedding or engagement may be announced. The card may indicate any situation where congratulations are the order of the day.

The fish (sometimes a winged one) appearing in the Page's cup represents an idea in the imagination, or an active imagination. This Page is all sweetness and light.

UPRIGHT PERSONALITY

Joyful, happy, good-natured, kind, and gentle, this character is very dreamy, but can be courageous when courage is called for. Has a deep interest in poetry and all the arts.

Example: A person who decides to take some (emotional) risk and isn't interested in being dissuaded. He or she "feels" it will all work out. The proverbial mercurial mind.

MESSAGE / NEWS

Birth, engagement, or marriage announcement.

REVERSED PERSONALITY

Inactive, moody, brooding, detached, oversensitive to anyone or anything seen as a threat.

Example: A person who uses deceptive behavior to blind you to his or her false intentions, or who plays carelessly with the emotions of others and is good at it. This character may use drugs or alcohol to escape reality.

MESSAGE / NEWS REVERSED
A reversed Page of Cups *and* the Empress in the same reading may mean health issues related to childbearing.

WORK: News about new appointments, accomplishments, an engagement, or an upcoming marriage.

LOVE: Love letters—the kind you keep in a box—mushy, gushy, or old, they still thrill you just the same.

MONEY: Your credit limit is raised—again. Suddenly your mail is addressed, "Preferred Customer."

FUTURE: Filter your many messages—discard most and read between the lines of the rest.

THE PAGE OF SWORDS

PAGE of SWORDS.

THIS IS A CARD ABOUT
HEEDING EARLY
WARNING SIGNALS.

You are being given advance notice, so be open and vigilant to the signs of change.

The Page stands on a windblown hilltop, poised as if on the alert; in one deck the page is running downhill right at you. What would you do if someone with a sharp sword came rushing at you? You'd probably duck or run—but pay attention! There is more to this Page than meets the eye!

UPRIGHT PERSONALITY

Very intelligent, a quick thinker; he has grace, dexterity, and an inquisitive mind. Always active, he seems to be possessed of boundless energy.

Example: The type of person who loves to talk, and seeks constant mental stimulation, for he or she gets bored easily. This person likes to "experiment" and take risks—which can cause problems for the self or for others.

MESSAGE / NEWS

Even in an upright state, the news the Page brings will be upsetting or unexpected.

REVERSED PERSONALITY

Unpredictable behavior leads to frustration. This character is capable of extreme and spiteful actions. The Page has fallen on his sword, and like a wounded animal, can lash out at others.

Example: The perpetual troublemaker at home or school, the office mole whom no one trusts—those who are able to best use communication skills in a negative manner.

MESSAGE / NEWS REVERSED

Expect the worst.

WORK: Use that sword like a baseball bat and hit a home run; don't strike out: you may soon have the opportunity to prove yourself.

LOVE: Someone may be using your relationship as if it were a game of skill or to prove something to someone else.

MONEY: Changes in your financial situation; look for a confidential note in your mailbox.

FUTURE: The situation is in flux; run for cover or jump in with both feet, but keep your head up and your eye on the ball!

THE PAGE OF PENTACLES

PAGE of PENTACLES.

THIS IS A CARD ABOUT
VISIONS, OMENS, AND
PREMONITIONS.

Messages come to you by nonmaterial means—a "gut" reaction.

The Page stands in a beautiful field of flowers; the Pentacle seems to float before him. The drape of his hat suggests a halo (angelic) or the "veil" of a psychic.

UPRIGHT PERSONALITY

The perpetual and dedicated student who loves to study and learn practical things. This person studies every angle before making a decision and is very goal–oriented.

Example: Teacher's pet, one who has great respect for authority.

MESSAGE / NEWS

A very informative message concerning the Querent's worldly ambitions.

REVERSED PERSONALITY

Rebellious and moody, this Page cannot seem to "follow through" on anything. He or she wants luxuries but doesn't want to work for them and cannot hold onto money.

Example: The "problem child" who rebels against parents, teachers, or any other authority figures. This character feels that the world owes him a living.

MESSAGE / NEWS REVERSED

Usually bad news about money matters or some form of disappointment. May also be an informative message the Querent refuses to heed.

WORK: The future is being defined and you are part of it; maybe there is even a little money in it for you.

LOVE: Someone shares your vision of the future: believe in it.

MONEY: You've got the position, raise, or grant, or you may have won something for your efforts.

FUTURE: The best of times is now. If it feels like your lucky day, believe it.

You might be asking, "So, John, where are the 'visions, omens, and premonitions' in here? Where does the 'psychic' come in?"

My feeling is that the more you know, the more you understand. As you increase your knowledge, your ability to "predict" an outcome improves. The universe is not random, but it is *ordered.* The clever Page of Pentacles may seem as though he is going by his "gut" reaction, when he is really mentally processing information so quickly he is unaware of what is going on. He may think he is "going with the flow," but the truth is that he *is* the flow—it is part of him ("Use the Force, Luke!"), and his random decisions are not so random after all. I'll be the first person to argue that the universe is not written in stone and we are blessed with free will, but an awareness of the future is the best way to prepare ourselves for dealing with it or adjusting it for optimal results. That is the purpose of divination.

THE KNIGHTS

Before we even start to discuss the Knights, take them out and look at them placed in this order (left to right)—Knight of Pentacles, Knight of Cups, Knight of Wands, Knight of Swords. Look at their horses and what the horses are doing:

> The Knight of Pentacles: his horse is standing completely still.
> The Knight of Cups: his horse is starting to walk or walking.
> The Knight of Wands: his horse is about to trot or canter.
> The Knight of Swords: his horse is charging at full gallop.

Knights, too, can bring messages and news, similar to the Pages. The appearance of a Knight or Knights in a reading usually indicates a long-term condition or life process that is about to change for the better or the worse—or end—and the horses indicate the speed of that process.

Here we see the full spectrum of possibilities, from a complete standstill with slow or no progress to a change happening so fast that it will possibly overpower, or run roughshod over, the Querent! These are the time indicators for the Knights.

As with all the Court cards, the Knights can also represent people and their personalities, and have both upright and reversed aspects. When reversed, consider that the Knight has fallen from his steed; all forward progress for better or worse is halted, and the Knight is very angry!

KNIGHTS

KNIGHT of WANDS.

KNIGHT of CUPS.

KNIGHT of SWORDS.

KNIGHT of PENTACLES.

THE KNIGHT OF WANDS

KNIGHT of WANDS.

THIS IS A CARD ABOUT
SPONTANEOUS CHANGES
OR IMPULSIVE BEHAVIOR.

You may need to become more aggressive in your approaches to your career, finances, or love life.

The Knight of Wands trots around here and there all over the landscape and seems to be in constant motion. In all things he can be a generous and passionate friend or lover, but his continual movement can create conflict or rivalry, since to others he may appear unclear about his direction.

UPRIGHT PERSONALITY

Hasty in all he does, he may be a young man who is a relative or a friend. He takes action where and when others would not. He tends to be hyperactive but controlled.

Example: A "Type A" workaholic who thrives on meeting another challenge, he may be a successful businessman or business partner, and a good father.

CHANGES

There is the possibility of a trip or travel—also a change of residence. The matter is going to be of great concern to the Querent.

REVERSED PERSONALITY

Disorganized, out-of-control, this character can be narrow-minded or absent-minded, and range from insecure to downright ornery!

Example: A "know-it-all" who is really resistant to change and wants to feel comfortable in all situations. He lacks the inner spark to get or keep going. He likes to feel important and has great ideas, but is antagonistic to the input of others.

CHANGES REVERSED

The situation is caused by inertia. Someone dropped the ball and no one is willing to pick it up.

WORK: Does the term "aggressive self-starter" apply to you? If you are a "follower," it is now time to act like a "leader."

LOVE: Someone is being actively pursued, or a relationship is moving much too fast.

MONEY: Don't wait if you feel a pressing need and you have no cash on hand—go out and charge it!

FUTURE: Something requires an immediate response; don't think too long, or at all.

THE KNIGHT OF CUPS

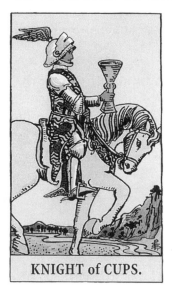

KNIGHT of CUPS.

THIS IS A CARD ABOUT
METHODICAL CHANGE
OR BEHAVIOR.

Someone is approaching you. His progress may be a bit slower than you would like, but the results will be memorable—perhaps even spectacular.

The Knight makes slow but definite progress as he rides over the countryside. He can represent the "knight in shining armor" of a young woman's dreams, for he can bear a love token or emotional message from himself or someone else. He is a person of high intelligence and deeply romantic, usually skilled in the arts.

UPRIGHT PERSONALITY

Genuinely honest, skilled in understanding human needs, he is willing to give his help—an excellent friend.

> *Example:* The card of the psychic. These people express themselves in color and symbol, not always in words. They are often counselors or therapists.

CHANGES

The change involves matters of deep emotional intensity for the Querent.

REVERSED PERSONALITY

A person who doesn't relate well to those around him and fears getting involved. (*Note*: it can also indicate someone who is indifferent to the Querent, even though the Querent is obsessed with him, or unrequited love.)

Example: Not a leader, but always a follower, this character is subject to any peer pressures that arise, and may be addicted to alcohol or drugs.

CHANGES REVERSED

The situation is caused by a lack of direction or clear purpose.

WORK: It may seem excruciatingly slow, but only incremental progress will achieve the required goals.

LOVE: Someone may attempt to sweep you off your feet. If things are moving too fast for you, slow them down.

MONEY: The check really is in the mail. Check your mailbox regularly!

FUTURE: Focus on the goal and its purpose, then the delivery method. Keep your eyes on the prize.

THE KNIGHT OF SWORDS

KNIGHT of SWORDS.

THIS IS A CARD ABOUT
ASSERTIVE BEHAVIOR OR
AGGRESSIVE CHANGES.

Something has gotten the adrenaline pumping and perhaps you are throwing caution to the wind.

The trees, sky, and clouds carry the feeling of motion into this card. The Knight, with sword flashing, charges into battle. If someone on horseback rushed at you with a drawn sword—what would your first reaction be? Someone is about to rush headlong into the Querent's life, or a change will happen so quickly that the Querent may not have time to prepare for it.

UPRIGHT PERSONALITY

Although courteous and kind, and with good intentions, this quick, sharp-witted knight expects others to be working on the same level as he. It could indicate that you are forcing your ideas on others, which is bringing you negative feedback and sometimes outright opposition.

Example: Jack-of-all-trades and master of none—yet his way is the only way.

CHANGES

The situation is caused by too narrow a focus; the Querent has become complacent and his or her world is about to be stirred up. In general, the Knight of Swords brings drastic news, and the change will be unsettling. If the Querent is expecting change, this may not be what he wants or expects.

REVERSED PERSONALITY

This character has difficulty in maintaining the strength, stamina, or mental attitude needed to see a situation through. He is argumentative for no apparent reason. It could indicate you have closed yourself off from a situation that desperately needs your attention.

> *Example:* The troublemaker who is always ready for a fight. The tyrant who is verbally abusive, and says things without thinking that hurt those most dear to him. He is hurting and you hurt along with him. He can be very secretive about his plans.

CHANGES REVERSED

The situation is caused by lack of direction, also delays, conflicts, and massive apprehension.

WORK: You tend to "make heads roll" to accomplish something. That "element of surprise" routine will only work so long before you get the backlash.

LOVE: Someone may be trying to break through your defenses. Make sure you don't get sidetracked.

MONEY: An unexpected problem causes major expenses that the Querent may not have the liquid cash to cover.

FUTURE: It's too late to look back, so cross the finish line and complete your mission.

THE KNIGHT OF PENTACLES

KNIGHT of PENTACLES.

THIS IS A CARD ABOUT RESPONSIBLE CHANGE AND DEFENSIVE BEHAVIOR.

A heavy man on a heavy horse stands in the middle of a freshly plowed field of possibilities, yet makes no effort to move. He stares placidly at the pentacle in his hand. Everything is calm and quiet.

UPRIGHT PERSONALITY

He is thorough, methodical, trustworthy, honest, stable—and also dull and unimaginative. Laborious and patient, he accepts responsibility graciously. Kind to animals, he loves nature.

Example: The type of person who invites you to his home and makes you feel as if it is your own. He is often a banker, investor, broker, farmer, or veterinarian, or has a job that is placid and not dynamic.

CHANGES

He suggests a situation involving departures, matters concerning money or land, or situations involving animals.

REVERSED PERSONALITY

Someone who is irresponsible and neglectful of his duties. He can't focus or commit, is very impatient, and can be timid or careless in his dealings. Not a person to be trusted.

Example: Someone who is frequently unemployed "through no fault of his own," or who has no interest in employment. While he may appear well-to-do, he doesn't know the value of a dollar. He may also exhibit a compulsive gambler mentality—expecting to make large gains without investment.

CHANGES REVERSED

Describes a situation dealing with an element of depression, inertia, or financial problems; also one caused by extreme materialism.

WORK: Be prepared—something is coming that will disturb your peace. Be ready and willing to fight for what is yours.

LOVE: Keep your guard up, since the situation may become risky, out of control, or contain an element of danger.

MONEY: There is probably nothing ominous hanging over your head, but don't be passive.

FUTURE: Someone calls your bluff and you know it, but you have to pretend he or she means business. Be serious about *your* intentions.

THE QUEENS AND KINGS

As with the Pages and Knights, the Queens and Kings also work on multiple levels, sometimes simultaneously.

The Queens and Kings usually represent people, either the Querent or some aspect of the Querent's personality, or someone entering or affecting the Querent's life at the moment. They can be parents, bosses, relations, or even total strangers that the Querent hasn't met (yet). They can also represent people the Querent looks to as counselors or confidants. As with the other Court cards, the Queens and Kings have differing and strong personalities, even within the same suit.

Queens and Kings also can represent *situations*, the way the Pages represent news and the Knights represent changes. When Court cards appear in a reading and their meaning is not readily apparent, I usually find it best to describe the personality type. That way, we see if they are someone the Querent knows, or

QUEENS

QUEEN of WANDS.

QUEEN of CUPS.

QUEEN of SWORDS.

QUEEN of PENTACLES.

whether their personality in some way reflects the Querent's current frame of mind. The Querent may be unaware that he or she is acting in a way that is different from normal, particularly if it is contrary to the usual pattern of behavior. In this case it may be a reflection of how others see or are interacting with the Querent.

These situations usually encourage the Querent to pursue a particular endeavor or caution against it. Sometimes these conditions are easy to decipher; at other times they can only be arrived at after some discussion with the Querent.

(At this point I'd like to note that there is nothing wrong with the reader asking questions of the Querent. Some people disagree with this, as though the reader were the "all-seeing, all-knowing" infallible oracle. Wouldn't you want to stay on the right track, rather than venture off in a totally wrong direction?)

Once again, although these cards may seem gender-specific, they do not have to be. When applied to the Querent, they can represent masculine or feminine qualities.

KINGS

KING of WANDS.

KING of CUPS.

KING of SWORDS.

KING of PENTACLES.

THE QUEEN OF WANDS

QUEEN of WANDS.

THIS IS A CARD ABOUT ENDURANCE, MAINTENANCE, AND SURVIVAL.

The Queen sits in state on her throne holding symbols of nature—her flowering Wand and a sunflower—which also appear on her throne. Some see her as a woman who lives in the country or is "close to nature." Much has been made of her black cat, a symbol of intuition, but also the "sinister" (meaning dishonest or evil) aspect of Venus! This aspect is more dominant when the card is reversed and the cat appears at the "top" of the card. Then it can usually be read as an indication of jealousy or infidelity. Her black cat represents her hedonistic, sensual, and passionate nature, qualities she shares with her cat.

UPRIGHT PERSONALITY

This Queen is affable, cordial, intelligent, a little aggressive, enthusiastic, motivated, and outgoing. Underlying her, though, is the element of Fire; she has a fiery temperament! Little flashes of this will appear even when she is in a good mood, so don't be surprised. As the Querent, she represents the qualities needed to succeed.

Example: She knows a great deal about many things and likes to share her knowledge with others.

SITUATION

This card indicates that now is a good time to move forward in a business venture.

REVERSED PERSONALITY

When reversed, we see the fiery temperament in all its glory. The Queen becomes forceful, overly temperamental, strict, and domineering. As the Querent, she is pushy and arrogant.

> *Example:* The person who says, "If we don't do this *my* way, I'm taking my bat and ball and going home." The lazy person who mops a floor because she is told to, but doesn't move anything and mops around the obstacles.

SITUATION REVERSED

This card is a discretionary warning to be careful in all business dealings—particularly with a woman, to avoid giving offense; and to beware of deception. (Remember that black cat!)

WORK: Go with the flow when you have to, but remember: if the situation comes to "do or die," it is the fittest that will survive. Some people work well in this type of situation and even flourish; you're probably one of them.

LOVE: A feeling of fertility grows strong, bringing a "need" to reproduce. Don't forget your birth control pills. This is another one of those pregnancy cards, so be discreet.

MONEY: Be astute—a wise investment at this time could pay handsomely.

FUTURE: A time to reap what was sown. Keep your wits about you.

THE QUEEN OF CUPS

QUEEN of CUPS.

THIS IS A CARD ABOUT
ANTICIPATION AND
FORESIGHT.

It deals with the ability to predict cycles, such as when to produce your best work or get the best results.

A beautiful Queen sits on her throne gazing intently at a very ornate cup (the only lidded cup in the deck). It is closed, indicating her thoughts are in the world of the unconscious, for she is very intuitive and has a great imagination. Tradition states that this Queen is a married woman with children, and a very good mother.

UPRIGHT PERSONALITY

Nurturing, sensitive, soft-spoken, and good-natured, this woman has a strong attachment to her family. Her devotion to them is stronger than her feelings for her friends, so if she has to choose she will support her family first. (Personally, I have always found this Queen to be a little shallow or superficial. She means well and wants to help you, as long as it's not inconvenient for her. On her bad days she can be a real whiner: "You need help *now*? I just did my nails!") As the Querent, she indicates that one should try to develop the more positive aspects of the card.

Example: She is often a nurse, doctor, counselor, preschool teacher, or veterinarian.

SITUATION

The situation is one concerning creativity and/or creative endeavors; these have a positive emotional tone.

REVERSED PERSONALITY

When reversed, this Queen will react first and think second; she is prone to emotional outbursts that seem unrelated to the situation she is in. She is always worrying and concerned about things over which she has no control. This card may indicate that the Querent is playing with circumstances—particularly psychic ones—which may have dangerous outcomes.

> *Example:* The addictive personality, one who uses an addiction to feel secure while in reality she is out of control. This card may indicate a teenage desire to delve into the paranormal in an attempt to control things or people.

SITUATION REVERSED

The situation is no longer under control. There is a need for counsel. Perhaps an outside source should be contacted to help correct the situation.

WORK: Those winds of change may already be blowing—don't get blown over (or away)! Make plans and watch for the signs that will best help you achieve them.

LOVE: Get in sync with your partner. Are you both thinking a short getaway may be the best thing? Get into a romantic cycle.

MONEY: Feeling rich and being rich are not the same thing. Don't spend that paycheck before you get it.

FUTURE: Do not attempt anything when all the conditions surrounding it seem to be telling you to wait.

THE QUEEN OF SWORDS

QUEEN of SWORDS.

THIS IS A CARD ABOUT
DOMINANCE AND
DOMINATION.

Getting your own way is a matter of great importance.

This frowning Queen sits on her throne holding her ever-present sword; she is beckoning someone in front of her to rise. Her attitude says, "I am the Queen *and you are not!*" Her tongue is as sharp as the sword she grasps, and she wields both with confidence. She is very good at sizing up people quickly and wastes no time or words in getting right to the point—her point, that is! She has seen tremendous sorrow and is usually perceived as a widow, is childless, or has lost a child.

UPRIGHT PERSONALITY

She has good leadership qualities, is very organized, and is a keen observer of people. She is able to contain her emotions when dealing with difficulties. As the Querent, she is a skillful communicator, but is seen as lacking in tact.

Example: "Lucy" of *Peanuts* fame or Joan Collins's Alexis Carrington on *Dynasty*.

SITUATION

The Querent is going through an emotionally devastating experience that he or she needs to use to become more spiritual.

REVERSED PERSONALITY

The reversed Queen is narrow-minded and overly judgmental. She is quick to criticize and everything she says is caustic to the point of cruelty. She refuses to listen to others and is easily angered if they don't listen to her. She can be sly, especially when she is being deceitful. As the Querent, her ability to make a clear judgment is compromised.

Example: She is the type of person you do *not* disclose details to; she will gather secret information against you, and then use it. Also, she will steal your ideas and then claim them as her own.

SITUATION REVERSED

The Querent is bogged down emotionally. The other cards in the spread will indicate a way out of this dilemma.

WORK: A powerful person blocks your realizations. Do not step out of line, for heads will roll. Self-preservation should come before self-sacrifice.

LOVE: This card indicates a person you may need to obtain permission from, or a marriage blessing, or parental consent. She might be the one that needs to give you an okay on a project. An upright card indicates that the answer is yes.

MONEY: A powerful person is involved and some "hoop jumping" will have to be done, especially if you are dependent on other people's money.

FUTURE: Play the part if you must, but being diplomatic will help turn a decision in your favor.

THE QUEEN OF PENTACLES

QUEEN of PENTACLES.

THIS IS A CARD ABOUT CONSIDERATION, UNDER-STANDING, AND BEING RESOURCEFUL, WHETHER YOU APPLY THESE QUALITIES TO OTHERS OR THE WORLD AROUND YOU.

This dark and powerful Queen sits on her throne among symbols of fertility and plenty. She is a very thoughtful and intelligent woman who applies herself in many creative ways. She is rich and charitable to others. Her only flaw is that she takes a long time to make decisions, and when she is in this state of contemplation, she appears moody or dismal in spite of herself. Sometimes this card is interchangeable with The Empress (see page 34).

UPRIGHT PERSONALITY

This Queen is creative, charitable, generous, quiet, and a responsible person. As the Querent, she is good in business, at gardening, and with children—even those who are not her own.

Example: Dirt doesn't stick to her; she has so much going for her in terms of happiness that she spreads it to others.

SITUATION

This Queen represents the harvest after much planning and labor; the acquisition of wisdom; and the prudent use of wealth.

REVERSED PERSONALITY

The Queen reversed is very insecure and becomes totally dependent on others to meet her own needs. She is prone to mood swings, mistrustful, and suspicious of others. As the Querent, she seems to be drowning, lost in her inability to do anything for herself.

Example: Addicted to money/spending, she does not want others to have more than she and will try to outdo you if she can—suck you in if she can't.

SITUATION REVERSED

This situation is one in which you need to exercise caution as to where and in whom you place your trust.

WORK: Being congenial helps maintain a pleasant atmosphere. Spread some indoor plants around.

LOVE: Use your romantic imagination—a picnic in the country-side, perhaps?

MONEY: Help a cause to get funded; donate money and time.

FUTURE: Seek an equitable solution whenever possible.

THE KING OF WANDS

KING of WANDS.

THIS IS A CARD ABOUT
CONTROL AND THE CHAIN
OF COMMAND.

You have accomplished a lot; a request is granted; or someone higher-up wants a word with you.

The King sits contemplating the horizon. Tradition says he is a married man with children and a "country gentleman." Like his Queen, he has a generous and passionate nature, but underneath it lurks a fiery temper and flashes of it may appear, even when he is calm.

UPRIGHT PERSONALITY

This man is proud, confident, enthusiastic, and kind, with excellent leadership qualities. He is nimble in mind and body. Sometimes his fiery temperament makes him hasty, but he will not steer you wrong.

Example: Someone intent on doing things his own way; however, you can depend on him to do them right the first time.

SITUATION

The situation is as it appears on the surface, with no hint of deception or problems. Good fortune is possibly coming your way and may appear from an unexpected source.

REVERSED PERSONALITY

When this King is off his throne, he is grumpy, pessimistic, and temperamental, lacks enthusiasm, and is quarrelsome. He also lacks confidence and may appear detached from his surroundings. His judgments are strict, unsympathetic, and might be prejudiced.

Example: The ultimate "time and talent" waster who spends his time trying to find others to do his tasks for him. He doesn't apply himself to the job at hand, or to anything he has no interest in.

SITUATION REVERSED

Someone is talking a good game, but the gloss is only a cheap veneer.

WORK: Call a quick meeting and discuss plans; you may be free to proceed, but get the necessary authorizations—just in case.

LOVE: Spend some time alone together, even if you have to schedule it on a calendar!

MONEY: Watch that bottom line. Keep those expenses down.

FUTURE: Develop your talent for judging character. If you become the boss, remember it is not a blank check that gives you your own way in all things.

THE KING OF CUPS

KING of CUPS.

THIS IS A CARD ABOUT
STAYING AFLOAT.

This king's throne is either floating on the turbulent ocean, or, like some decks, at the water's edge, battered by waves. Since water usually indicates the unconscious mind, this King is being battered from all sides by emotional troubles. However, the king is nonplussed by the situation, holding his own, and appears to be unconcerned about (but not ignorant of) the emotional tides around him. He covers his feelings with a calm exterior. Tradition says he is often involved in law, business, or even theology.

UPRIGHT PERSONALITY
This King is devout, and introspective. A man of great compassion, he is sensitive, considerate, and kind; he uses quiet power to make his point.

Example: Very strong but adaptable when the situation calls for it, he can adjust to almost anything and fit in just about anywhere.

SITUATION
Indications are that the situation will be received favorably, especially if it is an artistic pursuit.

REVERSED PERSONALITY

When this King is off his throne and dumped into the raging ocean, he becomes secretive. He may have problems expressing himself, or even express himself in conflicting emotions. His sense of perspective is lost, and some double-dealing may even come about.

Example: A jealous and possessive person with deep psychological problems, his mood changes from one moment to the next.

SITUATION REVERSED

Scandal. It may also indicate someone is trying to dump you, romantically or otherwise.

WORK: Grab a flotation device and ride out the waves. Keep your head about you, even if others are losing theirs.

LOVE: Someone may reveal his or her true colors. Be prepared to bail out—literally and figuratively.

MONEY: Hold onto the cash as long as you can.

FUTURE: Try to stay on top of things. Use your intuition when making decisions.

THE KING OF SWORDS

KING of SWORDS.

THIS IS A CARD ABOUT PATIENCE OR ENDURANCE.

This stern King sits on his throne while storm clouds gather about him. This man is as dull and emotionless as a statue; in fact, you will feel you might as well be talking to the rocks or a tree. All emotional outbursts from *you*, be they compassion or rage, are met with the same blank, lifeless eyes. If he looks at you (he may not), those eyes will bore through you as if you don't exist.

In his defense, this King is in the seat of the eternal judgment-maker, and he is carefully scrutinizing every element or detail of a situation before he speaks; he is more concerned that he will make a bad judgment call than you realize. Rather than speak incorrectly, he doesn't speak at all, much to the consternation of those around him. Unlike his Queen, who swings her Sword at everyone, the King just sits there. The phrase "lighten up" is not in this man's vocabulary.

Traditionally, this man is a judge of some kind, a military leader, or the CEO of a large corporation. He is firm but suspicious of those with whom he is unfamiliar.

UPRIGHT PERSONALITY

As a person, this King is well educated, fair and rational, logical, analytical, just, and honest. If this card represents you, you may be on the verge of a breakthrough about which you are now ready to communicate.

Example: A good lawyer, judge, or advisor. He will help you as long as you do what he tells you to do.

SITUATION
This card represents a situation that calls for clear thinking and clear expression, not haste.

REVERSED PERSONALITY
When this King falls on his Sword, he reacts strongly to everything (much like the Queen). He becomes hypercritical or cruel, insensitive and aloof. He can be cool and preoccupied when it comes to you, even appearing to be evil.

Example: The vicious, vindictive gossip. A person so totally self-absorbed that he doesn't care about anyone or anything as long as he gets what he wants.

SITUATION REVERSED
This card indicates a situation in which you are caught between two antagonistic persons and must navigate carefully; if it appears you are getting the favor of one, the other will attack you for it. The card can also indicate that judgments made against you seem unfair.

WORK: Learn to work within the system. Bucking it will get you fired.

LOVE: This relationship will take a lot of work, but if it endures, it will show lasting promise.

MONEY: You might consider investing in bonds or precious metals—something that lasts and is not prone to wild fluctuations.

FUTURE: It's lonely at the top! Remain alert and stay calm at all times. Think about the example of the "Sword of Damocles" suspended over your head by thin threads, hanging there but able to fall without notice. Keep your wits (and sense of humor) about you.

THE KING OF PENTACLES

KING of PENTACLES.

THIS IS A CARD ABOUT
BEING AT THE TOP.

This king sits comfortably on his ornate throne, surrounded by the wealth of the world. He is well dressed and a beautiful castle rises behind him. Perhaps you know someone who lives like a King, or at least thinks that the world should treat him like one. Tradition says this King has accomplished math skills and is often a banker. He is usually a reliable married man and has many children. He may also be a captain of industry or the owner of a large estate. His counsel will be of great help to the Querent.

UPRIGHT PERSONALITY

This King is thoughtful, methodical, responsible, solid, kind, generous, and industrious. He is well disposed toward the Querent.

Example: Good father/husband; the good provider who can manifest what he wants.

SITUATION

This card indicates that the Querent will meet with success in a worldly enterprise.

REVERSED PERSONALITY

When reversed, this King becomes stubborn (the Taurus influence) and indecisive. He wants security, but doesn't want to work for it. He can react harshly when unhappy. He is also very easy to bribe.

Example: A person who spends more than he can afford. He tends to buy material objects, because he wants them rather than needs them.

SITUATION REVERSED

This card indicates unfair competition (or he is treating the competition unfairly). It can indicate shady business practices.

WORK: Be on your best behavior if invited to a business luncheon with your boss. He is very willing to give you a nod of approval.

LOVE: Enjoy the success this arrangement brings to both of you.

MONEY: You have the finances available to enjoy the better things of life. You earned it, so spend it without qualms.

FUTURE: Seek someone with the right financial connections, or invest more financial resources to ensure the best results.

TAROT COMBINATIONS

AROT is more than merely memorizing the meanings of 156 upright and reversed cards. Once you become familiar with the cards, certain combinations of cards will start to develop new meanings for you, far beyond just the sum of the two cards.

When we speak of a card following or preceding another card, it is the card directly *following* or *preceding* (unless otherwise noted).

In proximity means there are other cards between the two cards of the combination, the closer the combination, the stronger the effect.

Surrounded, as in "surrounded by Pentacles," means the cards directly preceding and following that card are both Pentacles.

In any position refers to upright or reversed. We will deal with runs of cards (three Wands, four Kings, etc.) in the next section.

#0 The Fool (with)

Chariot #7—The Fool preceding the Chariot: important news is on the way.

Hermit #9—The Fool preceding the Hermit: a secret is being safely kept.
The Fool following the Hermit: something secret will be brought out into the open.

Wheel #10—The Fool preceding the Wheel of Fortune (a powerful, materialistic card): the qualities of the Fool are canceled out.

Devil #15—The Fool preceding the Devil (another powerful, materialistic card): the qualities of the Fool are canceled out.

Sun #19—The Fool preceding the Sun: happiness, enjoyment, and order coming from an unexpected source.

#1 The Magician

High Priestess #2—The Magician *reversed* preceding the High Priestess: occult powers have been misused.

Empress #3—The Magician following the Empress: discretion will bring success.

Lovers #6—The Magician following the Lovers: hesitation in beginning a new venture.
The Magician following the Lovers *reversed*: separation due to hesitation.

Wheel #10—The Magician and Wheel cards together: a change of job, residence, or life direction.
The Magician and the Wheel opposite each other in the fifth and tenth positions of a Celtic Cross spread: a delay.

Death #13—The Magician and Death following each other in any order cancel out each other's qualities.
The Magician and Death opposite each other in the fifth and tenth positions in a Celtic Cross spread (either order): an event will be canceled.

Devil #15—The Magician and the Devil opposite each other in the fifth and tenth positions of a Celtic Cross spread: a delay.

Star #17—The Magician following the Star: an excellent beginning for a project or artistic endeavor.

Judgment #20—Judgment *reversed* can mean loss or bitterness, but in proximity to the Magician, its influence is weakened.

World #21—The Magician and the World cards appearing together: material success.
If either or both are *reversed*: material success is negated.

#2 The High Priestess

Magician #1—The High Priestess following the Magician *reversed*: occult powers have been misused.

Hermit #9—The High Priestess following the Hermit: a secret will never be revealed.

The High Priestess preceding the Hermit: a secret will be discovered.

Wheel #10—The High Priestess and Wheel cards together: academic or artistic success in the offing. Next to each other *and* upright: a seemingly hopeless lawsuit will bring rewards for the Querent.

The High Priestess *reversed* and upright Wheel (in any order): loss of stability and possibly violent upheavals.

Justice #11—The High Priestess following Justice: secrets connected to laws will come to light.

The High Priestess preceding Justice: the meaning will be the same, but will be revealed only through legal dealings.

If both are reversed, justice may miscarry.

Temperance #14—The High Priestess *reversed* followed by upright Temperance: difficulty in finding a solution.

Tower #16—The High Priestess preceding the Tower: disaster in an established institution or in the sphere of religion.

If *both* of these cards are *reversed*: physical collapse or mental breakdown.*

#3 The Empress

Magician #1—The Empress preceding the Magician: discretion will bring success.

Chariot #7—The Empress preceding the Chariot: a decisive victory in material matters.

*Note: This information is provided in a historical and entertainment context only. It is *not* an attempt to diagnose or treat a medical condition. Refer a Querent with medical concerns to a physician.

The Empress *reversed* preceding the Chariot: delay, followed by inevitable victory.

Death #13—The Empress *reversed* followed by Death: the cards will cancel each other out.

Devil #15—The Empress *reversed* followed by the Devil: the cards will cancel each other out.

Tower #16—The Empress *reversed* followed by the Tower: the cards will cancel each other out.

Star #17—The Empress following the Star: a tranquil, happy existence.
The Empress preceding the Star: success is ensured through sustained effort powered by strong ambition.

Page of Cups—The Empress following the Page of Cups *reversed*: health issues related to childbearing.*

#4 The Emperor
Pentacles—The Emperor, surrounded by Pentacles: heavy responsibilities in connection with an offer from an authoritative person in high finance.

Hierophant #5—The Emperor and the Hierophant together: conflict between spiritual and temporal desires. The preceding card indicates the outcome.
The Emperor *reversed* following the Hierophant *reversed*: the failure of some enterprise.
The Emperor *reversed* preceding the Hierophant *reversed*: power and wealth lost by lack of wisdom.

Devil #15—The Emperor following the Devil: great social unrest.
The Emperor preceding the Devil: a threat to a world leader.

*Note: Again, this information is provided in a historical and entertainment context only. It is *not* an attempt to diagnose or treat a medical condition. Refer a Querent with medical concerns to a physician.

World #21—The Emperor preceding the World: a truce or peace, or a lull in a war.

The Emperor *reversed* preceding the World: loss of power or a conflict.

#5 The Hierophant

Emperor #4—The Hierophant and the Emperor together: a conflict between temporal and spiritual desires. The preceding card indicates the outcome.

The Hierophant *reversed* preceding the Emperor *reversed*: the failure of some enterprise.

The Hierophant *reversed* following the Emperor *reversed*: power and wealth lost through lack of wisdom.

Chariot #7 —The Hierophant following the Chariot: success in a creative endeavor.

Devil #15—The Hierophant and the Devil together cancel each other out; the "outcome" is determined from the surrounding cards.

#6 The Lovers

Swords—The Lovers followed by *any* Sword card: a relationship will end.

Magician #1—The Lovers preceding the Magician: hesitation in beginning a new venture.

The Lovers *reversed* before the Magician: a separation due to hesitation.

Chariot #7—The Lovers preceding the Chariot: betrayal.

The Lovers following the Chariot: the end of a romance or venture, or someone's sudden departure.

Death #13—The Lovers followed by Death: the end of a romantic attachment.

Temperance #14—The Lovers next to Temperance: romantic indecision.

The Lovers *reversed* next to Temperance: deceit on the part of one lover.

Moon #18—The Lovers following the Moon: the end of a love affair due to deception or lies, or because the love was illusory and not based in fact.

#7 The Chariot

Fool #0—The Chariot following the Fool: important news is on the way.

Empress #3—The Chariot following the Empress: a decisive victory in material matters.
The Chariot following the Empress *reversed*: delay followed by inevitable victory.

Hierophant #5—The Chariot preceding the Hierophant: success in a creative endeavor.

Lovers #6—The Chariot following the Lovers: betrayal.
The Chariot preceding the Lovers: the end of a romance or venture, or someone's sudden departure.

Strength #8—The Chariot preceding Strength: the Querent will show great strength in future trials.
The Chariot following Strength: considerable effort will be expended before triumph will occur.

Wheel #10—The Chariot and Wheel cards together: triumph.

Moon #18—The Chariot preceding the Moon: a secret will be brought to light.
The Chariot following the Moon: scandal or even illness.
The Chariot following the Moon *reversed*: a somewhat softened outcome.

Judgment #20—The Chariot following Judgment: fame and triumph.
The Chariot *reversed* following Judgment: the triumph will be short-lived because the sudden success will lead to weakness of character.

World #21—The Chariot preceding the World: ambitions will be fulfilled.

#8 Strength

This card is so powerful that it influences every card in the spread. The Strength card adds force to any Major Arcana card.

Chariot #7—Strength following the Chariot: the Querent will show great strength in future trials.

Strength preceding the Chariot: a considerable amount of effort will be expended before the inevitable triumph.

Death #13—Strength followed by Death: a serious but nonfatal illness.*

Strength following Death: an abrupt ending of something.

Strength *reversed* following Death *reversed*: a narrow escape.

Tower #16—Strength preceding the Tower increases the Tower's impact.

#9 The Hermit

Fool #0—The Hermit following the Fool: a secret will be kept safely.

The Hermit preceding the Fool: something secret will be brought out into the open.

High Priestess #2—The Hermit preceding the High Priestess: a secret will never be revealed.

The Hermit following the High Priestess: a secret will be discovered.

Wheel #10—The Hermit and Wheel cards together: a sign of lasting good fortune.

Devil #15—The Hermit following the Devil: the dark power will predominate.

The Hermit preceding the Devil: good will prevail as the Hermit's light shines on powerful enemies or devious methods.

The Hermit *reversed* in either case: delays the outcome.

*Note: This information is provided in a historical and entertainment context *only*. It is *not* an attempt to diagnose or treat a medical condition. Refer a Querent with medical concerns to a physician.

Judgment #20—The Hermit following Judgment: inner spirituality will triumph.

The Hermit *reversed* following Judgment: discoveries made by others will be of great advantage when revealed to the Querent.

World #21—The Hermit and the World cards appearing together: spiritual success.

If either or both are *reversed*: the spiritual success is negated.

#10 The Wheel of Fortune

Fool #0—The Wheel (a powerful, materialistic card) following the Fool: the qualities of the Fool are canceled out.

Magician #1—The Wheel and the Magician cards together: a change of job, residence, or life direction.

High Priestess #2—The Wheel and the High Priestess cards together: academic or artistic success. A seemingly hopeless lawsuit will bring rewards to the Querent.

The Wheel and the High Priestess *reversed* (any order): loss of stability and possibly violent upheavals.

Chariot #7—The Wheel and the Chariot cards together: triumph.

Hermit #9—The Wheel and the Hermit cards together: a sign of lasting good fortune.

Judgment #20—The Wheel following Judgment *reversed*: a fear of personal ruin, but its influence is weakened by proximity to the Wheel.

World #21—The Wheel and the World cards together: light will be shed on a hidden factor that will bring success.

#11 Justice

The High Priestess #2—Justice preceding the High Priestess: secrets connected to laws will come to light.

Justice following the High Priestess: the meaning will be the same, but will be revealed only through legal dealings.

If both are *reversed*, justice may miscarry.

Hanged Man #12—Justice preceding the Hanged Man: tolerance should be shown—not harsh judgments.

Temperance #14—Justice following Temperance: a just end to a lengthy legal process.
Justice preceding Temperance: legal delays.
Justice preceding Temperance *reversed*: an end to hesitation.

Devil #15—Justice following the Devil indicates a miscarriage of justice.
Justice preceding the Devil: an incriminating charge will prove false.

Moon #18—Justice and the Moon next to each other: a strong malevolent situation implying unjust dealings or deceit.

World #21—Justice and the World appear together: completion and reward.
If either or both are *reversed*, the reward is negated.

#12 The Hanged Man
Justice #11– The Hanged Man following Justice: tolerance should be shown—not harsh judgments.

Death #13—The Hanged Man and Death (in either order): regret over the end of a situation, or a major sacrifice must be made.

Temperance #14—The Hanged Man and Temperance (in either order) together: deceit, lies, and indecision.

Devil #15—The Hanged Man and the Devil appearing together (in either order): a bond, a partnership, or even a marriage in which one partner is selfish and must be prepared to give more, while the other partner makes a major sacrifice to maintain the commitment.

World #21—The Hanged Man following the World: a sacrifice that may end in sadness and a parting.
The Hanged Man preceding the World: a loving sacrifice will bring about a triumph.

#13 Death

Magician #1—Death and the Magician following each other in any order cancel out each other's qualities.

Death and the Magician opposite each other in the fifth and tenth positions in a Celtic Cross spread (either order): an event will be canceled.

Empress #3—Death following the Empress *reversed*: the cards cancel each other out.

Lovers #6—Death following the Lovers: the end of a romantic attachment.

Strength #8—Death following Strength: usually a serious but nonfatal illness.*

Death followed by Strength: an abrupt ending to something.

Death *reversed* followed by Strength *reversed*: a narrow escape.

Hanged Man #12—Death and the Hanged Man (in either order): regret over the end of a situation, or a major sacrifice must be made.

Tower #16—Death and the Tower together in either order: an impending crisis or disaster.

If the Tower is *reversed*: a narrow escape from misfortune.

Moon #18—Death following the Moon: loss from slander.

If both cards are *reversed*: the truth will be discovered.

Sun #19—Death following the Sun: success through something coming to an end.

World #21—Death preceding the World: the fall of a world leader or his government, or a worldwide medical epidemic.

Note: This information is provided in a historical and entertainment context only. It is *not* an attempt to diagnose or treat a medical condition. Refer a Querent with medical concerns to a physician.

#14 Temperance

High Priestess #2—Temperance following the High Priestess *reversed*: difficulty in finding a solution.

Lovers #6—Temperance next to the Lovers: romantic indecision.
Temperance next to the Lovers *reversed*: deceit on the part of one lover.

Justice #11—Temperance preceding Justice: a just end to a lengthy legal process.
Temperance following Justice: legal delays.
Temperance *reversed* following Justice: an end to hesitation.

Hanged Man #12—Temperance and the Hanged Man together (in either order): deceit, lies, and indecision.

#15 The Devil

Fool #0—The Devil (a powerful, materialistic card) following the Fool: the qualities of the Fool are canceled out.

Magician #1—The Devil and the Magician opposite each other in the fifth and tenth positions of a Celtic Cross spread: a delay.

Empress #3—The Devil following the Empress *reversed*: the cards cancel each other out.

Emperor #4—The Devil preceding the Emperor: great social unrest.
The Devil following the Emperor: a threat to a world leader.

Hierophant #5—The Devil and the Hierophant cancel each other out; the "outcome" is determined by the surrounding cards.

Hermit #9—The Devil preceding the Hermit: the Devil's dark power will predominate.
The Devil following the Hermit: good shall prevail, as the Hermit's light shines on powerful enemies or devious methods.
The Hermit *reversed* in either case: delays the outcome for a time.

Justice #11—The Devil preceding Justice: a miscarriage of justice.
The Devil following Justice: an incrimination will prove false.

Hanged Man #12—The Devil and the Hanged Man appearing together (in either order): a bond, partnership, or marriage in which one partner is selfish and needs to give more, while the other partner makes a major sacrifice to maintain the commitment.

Star #17—The Devil with the Star in any position: they cancel each other out.

Moon #18—The Devil and the Moon next to each other: a strongly antagonistic situation, implying deceit by another.

Judgment #20—The Devil upright with Judgment *reversed* can mean transient success, but the degree of the success is weakened by its proximity to the Devil card.

#16 The Tower
High Priestess #2—The Tower following the High Priestess: disaster in an established institution or in the sphere of religion.
If both cards are *reversed*: physical collapse or mental breakdown.*

Empress #3—The Tower following the Empress *reversed*: the cards cancel each other out.

Strength #8—The Tower following Strength: increase in the Tower's impact.

Death #13—The Tower and Death together (in either order): an impending crisis or disaster.
The Tower *reversed*: a narrow escape from misfortune.

Moon #18—The Tower and the Moon next to each other: a hostile situation implying deceit by another.

Sun #19—The Tower preceding the Sun: good shall come out of evil, and what first appeared as a catastrophe will become an advantage.

Note: This information is provided in a historical and entertainment context only. It is *not* an attempt to diagnose or treat a medical condition. Refer a Querent with medical concerns to a physician.

World #21—The Tower following the World: the Tower's impact is softened.

#17 The Star
Magician #1—The Star preceding the Magician: an excellent beginning for a project or artistic endeavor.

Empress #3—The Star preceding the Empress: a tranquil, happy existence.
The Star following the Empress: success is ensured through sustained effort powered by strong ambition.

Devil #15—The Star with the Devil in any position: they cancel each other out.

#18 The Moon
Lovers #6—The Moon preceding the Lovers: the end of a love affair due to deception or lies, or because the love was illusory and not based in fact.

Chariot #7—The Moon following the Chariot: a secret is brought to light.
The Moon preceding the Chariot: scandal or even illness.
The Moon *reversed* preceding the Chariot: the outcome will be softened somewhat.

Justice #11—The Moon and Justice next to each other: a strongly malevolent situation implying unjust dealings or deceit.

Death #13—The Moon followed by Death: loss from slander.
If *both* cards are *reversed*, the truth will be discovered.

Devil #15—The Moon and the Devil next to each other: a strongly antagonistic situation implying deceit by another.

Tower #16—The Moon and the Tower next to each other: a hostile situation implying deceit by another.

#19 The Sun

Two of Cups—The Sun with the Two of Cups: two happy people will share a lasting, loving partnership.

Fool #0—The Sun following the Fool: happiness, enjoyment, and order coming from an unexpected source.

Death #13—The Sun preceding the Death card: success through something coming to an end.

Tower #16—The Sun following the Tower: good will come out of evil, and what first appeared a catastrophe will become an advantage.

World #21—The Sun next to the World: an uplifting experience that will bring harmony, joy, and love.

#20 Judgment

Magician #1—Judgment *reversed* can mean loss or bitterness, but its influence is weakened by proximity to the Magician.

Chariot #7—Judgment preceding the Chariot: fame and triumph.
If the Chariot is *reversed*: the triumph will be short-lived, because the sudden success will reveal weakness of character.

Hermit #9—Judgment preceding the Hermit: a triumph of inner spirituality.
If the Hermit is *reversed*: discoveries made by others will be of great advantage when revealed to the Querent.

Wheel #10—Judgment *reversed*: a fear of ruination, but this card's influence is weakened by proximity to the Wheel.

Devil #15—Judgment *reversed* can mean transient success, but the degree of success is weakened by its proximity to the Devil card.

#21 The World

Magician #1—The World and the Magician together: material success.

If either or both are *reversed*: material success is negated.

Emperor #4—The World following the Emperor: a truce or peace, or a lull in a war.
If the Emperor is *reversed*: a loss of power, or conflict.

Chariot #7—The World following the Chariot: ambitions will be fulfilled.

Hermit #9—The World and the Hermit together: spiritual success.
If either or both are *reversed*: the spiritual success is negated.

Wheel #10—The World and the Wheel together: light will be shed on a hidden factor that will bring success.

Justice #11—The World and Justice together: completion and reward.
If either or both are *reversed*: the reward is negated.

Hanged Man #12—The World preceding the Hanged Man: a sacrifice that may end in sadness and a parting.
The World following the Hanged Man: a loving sacrifice will bring about a triumph.

Death #13—The World following the Death card: the fall of a world leader or his government, or a worldwide medical epidemic.

Tower #16—The World preceding the Tower softens the Tower's impact.

Sun #19—The World next to the Sun: an uplifting experience that will bring harmony, joy, and love.

RUNS OF SUITS, NUMBERS, AND CARDS

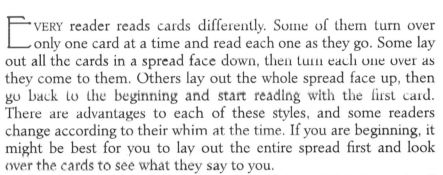

EVERY reader reads cards differently. Some of them turn over only one card at a time and read each one as they go. Some lay out all the cards in a spread face down, then turn each one over as they come to them. Others lay out the whole spread face up, then go back to the beginning and start reading with the first card. There are advantages to each of these styles, and some readers change according to their whim at the time. If you are beginning, it might be best for you to lay out the entire spread first and look over the cards to see what they say to you.

Sometimes the cards seem to reveal nothing. With the cards all face up you can look for trends or runs in the cards, and start your reading from that standpoint. This may be the best way to start when you have a difficult reading facing you—because you've "blanked out." Even experienced card readers can draw a blank after laying out ten cards!

A "run" of cards is three or more of some particular aspect of the cards. They do not have to lie next to each other, and they can be anywhere in the spread to be considered a run. For example, I have gotten a run of all four Queens in a *spread*, but the odds of getting four Queens in a *row* are almost impossible.

Major Arcana Cards

For example, in the classic Celtic Cross spread, there are 10 cards; if three or more of them in the spread are Major Arcana cards, it is considered a run of Majors. Most readers consider this particular condition to be "strong," whereas a Celtic Cross spread with only one or two Major Arcana cards is considered weak. With 22 Major and 56 Minor cards, the chances of getting three or more

Major Arcana cards are not especially good, but not surprising. This is one reason some readers use only the Majors and skip the Minors.

Runs of Suits

After you have considered the number of Major Arcana in the reading (and the positions they fall into), you might next see whether there are any runs of the suits. Again, three or more of a suit in the spread is considered a run, even if they are not next to each other.

In the ten cards in the Celtic Cross spread there can be up to three different types of runs—so take a good look.

A run of Wands usually indicates that the situation is primarily in the realm of thought, or in the very first stages of development.

A run of Cups usually indicates that the situation is felt primarily in the realm of emotion or spirit, but not necessarily manifested outwardly.

A run of Pentacles usually indicates that the situation or condition is starting to take form, or is in the process of being demonstrated.

A run of Swords predicts tremendous activity, agitation, or acceleration because Swords show the last stages of effort before the final result.

Runs of Numbers

Next, you might see if you have any runs of numbers, including the Major Arcana numbers. As in numerology, remember to add the two digits of a two-digit number together and reduce whenever possible. Thus a 10 can be read as 10 or 1 (1 + 0 = 1), Temperance as 5 (1 + 4 = 5), and the World as 3 (2 + 1= 3).

Note: The following section on runs of pip cards is a compilation but borrows heavily from Arthur Waite's *The Key to the Tarot*, which was first published in 1910. The style and lexicon of his time is quite stifling, and trying to ascertain what Waite actually meant is sometimes difficult. Occasionally, it is impossible to find a companion word in modern English usage. The fact that he may have deliberately used misleading terms to confuse the uninitiated adds to the vagueness of the language. Unfortunately for us in the 21st century, Waite never revealed what is true and what is deception.

Another problem: what we consider to be the main interpretation of the cards might not even apply when multiples of them appear in a reading—many appear to be contradictory! Thus, Eights—which we consider to be positive changes—might indicate a setback if four of them appear—and upright at that!

Also, multiples of cards appearing in the reversed position might have positive meanings.

Aces

A run of Ones (Aces) indicates that a situation is about to begin or is in the beginning stages:

Upright
4 Ones: favorable, profitable, or auspicious chance
3 Ones: a small or abbreviated success
2 Ones: collusion, trickery, or betrayal

Reversed
4 Ones: downfall, dishonor, personal insults
3 Ones: corruption, seduction, debauchery
2 Ones: enemies, opponents, rivals

Ace of Pentacles in a run of Wands: quick thinking will benefit your finances.
Ace of Pentacles in a run of Cups: emotional problems delay a business project.
Ace of Pentacles in a run of Swords: obstacles invade an ambitious project.

Ace of Wands in a run of Pentacles: an increase in your status or wealth, or both.
Ace of Wands in a run of Cups: financial growth brings a sense of joy.
Ace of Wands in a run of Swords: loss of personal wealth.

Ace of Cups in a run of Pentacles: romance encountered on a journey, or at work.
Ace of Cups in a run of Wands: you will receive or disburse a generous gift.
Ace of Cups in a run of Swords: serious setbacks befall a love affair.

Ace of Swords in a run of Pentacles: plans are withdrawn or
  curtailed suddenly.
Ace of Swords in a run of Cups: emotional conflict comes to the fore.
Ace of Swords in a run of Wands: financial matters come to a head.

Twos

A run of Twos indicates a waiting period where there will be at
least partial success, but more will be revealed later. Many twos can
also indicate a reconciliation, a reunion, and/or an element of surprise.

Upright

4 Twos: a relationship ends but a new one awaits
3 Twos: partnership flourishes
2 Twos: partnership separates

Reversed

4 Twos: compromise, negotiation, appeasement
3 Twos: trepidation, anxiety, concern
2 Twos: suspicion, doubt, skepticism

Threes

A run of Threes indicates group activities or situations involving
more than one person. Many Threes can also indicate delay, but
with the promise of future success.

Upright

4 Threes: happiness, but don't become smug
3 Threes: easy success and good fortune
2 Threes: promising outlook

Reversed

4 Threes: achievement, accomplishment, great success
3 Threes: serenity, tranquility, peacefulness
2 Threes: safety, reliability, security

Fours

A run of Fours indicates fruition or the manifestation of an
idea, along with the foundation or space where things can grow.

Upright

4 Fours: equality, stability

3 Fours: sudden inspiration

2 Fours: stalemate

Reversed

4 Fours: much traveling by foot

3 Fours: sense of foreboding, restlessness, anxiety.

2 Fours: disagreement, dispute, argument

Fives

A run of Fives indicates change, challenge, and fluctuations—favorable or unfavorable. Many Fives may also indicate material prosperity, but spiritual poverty if not properly balanced or understood.

Upright

4 Fives: order, uniformity

3 Fives: determination

2 Fives: a need for vigilance, caution, forethought

Reversed

4 Fives: harmony, union, agreement

3 Fives: procrastination, hesitation, delay

2 Fives: incompatibility, adversity

Sixes

A run of Sixes indicates adjustments in thought, attitudes, or conditions. Many Sixes indicate the ability to transcend difficulties.

Upright

4 Sixes: abundance, exuberance, generosity

3 Sixes: success, prosperity, achievement

2 Sixes: irritability, agitation, bitterness

Reversed

4 Sixes: anxiety, anguish, distress

3 Sixes: atonement, compensation, amends

2 Sixes: collapse, downfall, ruin

Sevens

A run of Sevens indicates a period of introspection or solitude. Many Sevens can also indicate advantages or gains that come through unexpectedly.

Upright
    4 Sevens: complications, manipulations, intrigue
    3 Sevens: illness, debility
    2 Sevens: notification, news, information forthcoming

Reversed
    4 Sevens: quarrels, controversy, contradiction
    3 Sevens: joy, enthusiasm, festivities
    2 Sevens: persons of no character

Eights
    A run of Eights indicates a positive change of mind or status—the beneficial qualities of the number eight rarely get diluted.

Upright
    4 Eights: a setback, misfortune, unexpected delays
    3 Eights: marriage, union, or merger
    2 Eights: new insight or knowledge

Reversed
    4 Eights: misunderstanding, error, fallacy.
    3 Eights: a revelation, spectacle, or phenomenon
    2 Eights: troubles, misfortune, calamity

Nines
    A run of Nines indicates that situations or events are nearing completion, or have just been completed and another plateau waits.

Upright
    4 Nines: a good friend
    3 Nines: accomplishment
    2 Nines: acceptance

Reversed
    4 Nines: getting taken, extortion
    3 Nines: indiscretion, lacking in judgment or caution
    2 Nines: a small improvement or profit

Tens
    A run of Tens can be read the same as the number one;

however, Tens signify a cyclical beginning and/or a time when you may have to come to grips with something you have avoided in the past.

Upright
4 Tens: censure, criticism
3 Tens: a new phase beginning
2 Tens: modification

Reversed
4 Tens: event or happening about to take place
3 Tens: disappointment, situation not as anticipated
2 Tens: expectation fulfilled

RUNS OF COURT CARDS

Pages

Upright
4 Pages: infirmity
3 Pages: disagreement or dispute
2 Pages: restlessness

Reversed
4 Pages: deprivation, confiscation, a refusal
3 Pages: idleness, unemployment—but also a vacation!
2 Pages: a partnership

Knights

Upright
4 Knights: serious matters or changes
3 Knights: verbal sparring or a lively debate
2 Knights: fraternity, intimacy

Reversed
4 Knights: alliance, partnership, or establishment of a new business
3 Knights: personal encounter, confrontation, or clash
2 Knights: weakness, gullibility, or susceptibility

Queens

Upright
4 Queens: a great debate
3 Queens: deception, hypocrisy
2 Queens: sincere friends (male or female)

Reversed
4 Queens: bad company
3 Queens: gluttony or greed
2 Queens: drudgery, toil, work

The Queen of Swords coming between a King and another Queen can be a deceitful woman coming between husband and wife.

Kings

Upright
4 Kings: recognition or commendation
3 Kings: conference, deliberation, an interview
2 Kings: consultation, an opinion being offered

Reversed
4 Kings: haste, acceleration
3 Kings: negotiation, reciprocity, transacting business
2 Kings: schemes, strategies, projects

Any number of mixed Court cards indicates a gathering of people or a festive occasion.

LIFE CARDS

WHILE consulting the cards, I often find that we ourselves stand in the way of our achieving our needs and wants, but we are not aware that we are doing it. Reading the Tarot invariably points us toward awareness, spiritual growth, and understanding. Another way to use the Tarot is to determine our Life cards—our soul, personality, and shadow cards—and to study and reflect on them. Many seekers find that by working with these cards, they discover invaluable information about themselves.

Earlier in this book I said that Tarot was "of the moment," meaning the moment you shuffle the cards for a particular reading. The next time you ask a question, the cards will be about that particular moment. Since your birth date is an *exact* moment—the start of your life—your Life cards reflect the essence of you in this lifetime. You can find them by combining a bit of numerology with the Tarot. Just reduce your birth date to *a single digit*. Your soul card is the corresponding card from the Major Arcana of the Tarot.

Before we go further, I need to explain something. Tarot and numerology are two completely and separately developed systems, although they do overlap. In Tarot, for example, the number five deals with instability, but in numerology, five deals with freedom and expansion. Once you take a set of parameters from one system and impose the limitations of another system over them, quirks appear. Some need to be accepted at face value: there are only 21 positive numbers in the Major Arcana but an infinite number of possible integers. This results in some birth numbers having three cards, some only two.

Tarot developed over the course of centuries, and the people who manipulated Tarot according to their own understanding did not necessarily have a background in what the numbers are supposed to mean. Numbers are constant; you can "bend" the meaning of a Tarot card more easily than you can make a positive number into a negative one! Hopefully, this somewhat confusing sentence will make more sense as you read on, for numerology is a consuming process, just as Tarot can be, and in this chapter I am limiting our discussion to these two techniques.

For an example of the reduction process, my birth date is May 12, 1955. Adding the digits together, $5+1+2+1+9+5+5 = 28$, and $2 + 8 = 10$. $1 + 0 = 1$, so my soul card is the Magician. If you wish to check your math, add your birth date up again this way:

$$
\begin{array}{l}
05 \\
12 \\
\underline{1955} \\
1972
\end{array} = 1 + 9 + 7 + 2 \ = 19; \ 1 + 9 = 10; \ 1 + 0 = 1
$$

Our soul card represents those qualities we aspire to—our soul's hopes, desires, goals, and dreams. It also defines us, the way our astrological signs show us our differences. Our personality card reflects how we appear to the world. As for the shadow card—it represents those qualities we most like to ignore—the bits we don't like about ourselves. For example, the Star as shadow would indicate a tendency to ignore unconscious signals and to refuse to see the bright side. Basically, if we think in terms of the reversed card meanings for our shadow, we won't go too far wrong. As I said, these cards are for us to study, meditate, and reflect upon.

If your birth number is 1, your soul card is 1—The Magician; your personality card is 10—The Wheel of Fortune; and your shadow card is 19—The Sun.

If you have the Soul of a Magician, you can make whatever it is you need—or desire to have happen in your life—work out the way you would like. This will take a little planning, a little manipulation, and a *lot* of determination. Your personality is the Wheel, which does spin, and chance sometimes does not fall the way you wish it would. Being a Magician, you should be able to deal with the problems as long as you don't seek to control every situation. The Sun as your shadow says that you need to look for the "silver lining," even during a downpour (which the Wheel can easily bring you).

However, as the Magician, you have the ability to make the situation work, adapt to the changes, and deal with the fearful or pessimistic parts of yourself.

If your birth number is 2, your soul card is 2—The High Priestess; your personality card is 11—Justice (or Strength); and your shadow card is 20—Judgment.

With the soul of a High Priestess, your intuitive processes influence everything you do, even unconsciously. You know what people have done before they tell you. This complements your personality, where you seek justice, looking for fairness in everything you do and in how you deal with the world. This can cause you to seem an enigma to some, and truly mysterious to others. The Judgment card as your Shadow, however, cautions you to be careful and not to misuse your abilities or rush to judgment.

If your birth number is 3, your soul card is 3—The Empress; your personality card is 12—The Hanged Man; and your shadow card is 21—The World.

With the Empress as your soul card, you are the very essence of the Earth Mother—wishing the best and giving the best to everyone; you are very outgoing in nature. Your personality of the Hanged Man is a further extension of the Empress: you will go to great lengths to find the "little bit of good" in everyone, and even turn your life or beliefs upside down to accommodate others. The World as your shadow, though, is a reminder that people will disappoint you from time to time. Accept their faults graciously but don't let them take advantage of you.

If your birth number is 4, your soul and personality cards are 4—The Emperor; your shadow card is 13—Death.

With the soul and personality of an Emperor, you usually look for the best and strongest to help you in caring for "the good of the whole." You tend to be disciplined, grounded, and practical. You are shadowed by the Death card, which brings changes, but most of these may be used as opportunities for growth and development. Don't be blind to the fact that change is good, and development is an ongoing process. The rock mountain that you have created will be eroded by time, so plan for the future while maintaining the present. What you build may be lasting, but it cannot be eternal.

If your birth number is 5, your soul and personality cards are 5—The Hierophant; your shadow card is 14—Temperance.

With the Hierophant, your soul strives to maintain what already exists. Your personality seeks to help others, but is usually conservative in nature and response. Sometimes this behavior makes you anxious because you see the need for expansion, but do not want to take risks. The Temperance shadow kicks you off your throne and tells you to be more original instead of predictable, and to become more active and develop a sense of adventure, because you need to balance your restrictive behavior. The key to your development will be to accept small changes as helpful instead of disruptive.

If your birth number is 6, your soul and personality cards are 6—The Lovers; your shadow card is 15—The Devil.

Your Lovers soul says that you surround yourself with harmony, have passionate ideals, and enjoy the equilibrium that sharing brings to your life. You have an instinctive understanding of what makes things "tick." Your devotion to others is probably the first thing that people notice about you. However, the Devil card, a card of excesses and abuses, shadows you. You are being warned to be careful of those who will seek to take advantage of your good nature, those who try to manipulate you to their ends. It also warns you not to meddle in the affairs of others under the guise of helping them. Everyone needs to find his or her own balance, so enjoy your friends and hobbies, but do not use love to try to control others.

If your birth number is 7, your soul and personality cards are 7—The Chariot; your shadow card is 16—The Tower.

You are passionate, responding to the rhythms of life, jumping in with both feet. You maintain a balance between the intellectual, mystical, and philosophical, cramming more activity into a span of time than those around you, which can confuse and confound them. At times you contradict yourself, embracing both ends of the spectrum but not the center. Those who can keep up with you know that life with you will never be complacent or boring. The Tower as your shadow means you can become moody or even pessimistic, tending to discard those who cannot maintain your speed or work on your level. It tells you to listen to and even occasionally to obey the wishes of others, for they bring lessons for you to learn. Learn to cooperate with others more often instead of running off to do things your way.

If your birth number is 8, your soul and personality cards are 8—Strength (or Justice); your shadow card is 17—The Star.

You are a pillar of Strength for those seeking strength and you have an air of justice about you. You are always in control of yourself, and are not unsettled by events that may attempt to chip away at your determined facade. You understand that a few setbacks may be necessary to gain a foothold, but your very capable hands are guided by your very capable intellect. However, the Star warns you against being too aggressive, which may blind you into believing that Strength will conquer all. That mindset would make you zealous, develop militant beliefs, or bring you to a greedy or a materialistic outlook. Authority should be balanced with justice.

If your birth number is 9, your soul and personality cards are 9—The Hermit; your shadow card is 18—The Moon.

Your universal awareness coupled with selflessness and courage show you to be a humanitarian. You have sought the answers in an attempt to find your purpose in life, and you seek to teach others to help them understand the enjoyment of silent meditation, the beauty of a long walk in the woods, or the joys of self-discovery. Solitude is everything to you, so you tend to limit your interaction with others to short though intense moments in time. The shadow of the Moon crosses your path to remind you that everything is a cycle, and you must sometimes move backward in order to move forward. You need to balance your need for deep thoughts with human interaction, sharing what you have learned with others. In that way all can continue to grow.

YEAR CARD

OU can use the same numerological process to determine the kind of year you will have. Figure out your year card the same way as you would your soul card, but use the year you want to know about instead of your birth year. Unlike the example for your birth number, *do not reduce any two-digit number* unless the number is 22 or higher, since we want to use the full set of 21 numbered Major Arcana cards. Also, in this exercise, add the numbers in columns, not linearly.

The best example I can provide is my own experience with the year 2002. Take my birthday of 05-12-2002 and reduce it in this manner:

    05
    12
    2002
    ─────
    2019 = 2 + 0 + 1 + 9 = 12—The Year of the Hanged Man

Well! Let me tell you! That twelve-month period between birthdays lived up to every aspect of the Hanged Man that you can imagine! I literally went *nowhere* that year. In 2002 I tried to sell the manuscript for this book, and although I met with enthusiasm—there were even a few takers—the manuscript sat in limbo. At one point I even thought about self-publishing it, but was determined to believe in the strength of my writing. There was nothing I could do but hang there—*and* hang in there—which is why you are reading this book today.

Now—an interesting thing happened. To check my math I added the same date in a line and still got a 12 for 2002:

$$5 + 1 + 2 + 2 + 0 + 0 + 2 = 12$$

So logic told me that for the next year all I needed to do was add 1 and the next year (2003) would be 13—Death—the card of changes. Selling the book would definitely bring changes in my life, so a 13 for 2003 seemed right. I was explaining this to my spiritual counselor and she corrected me, saying that I should use only the columnar addition process for the Year Card exercise because:

$$\begin{array}{r} 05 \\ 12 \\ \underline{2003} \\ \mathbf{2020} \end{array}$$ = 2 + 0 + 2 + 0 = 4—The Emperor! The card of male power.

Now, you can probably argue that both of these cards can and will indicate my future, possibly in tandem. Since 13 does reduce to 4 (even though we are not supposed to reduce a number 21 or less), I am going to take my counselor's suggestion and say that to determine your year card, add the figures in columns and not in a linear way. (People who study numerology are VERY specific as to what math formula is used to determine which number.) It will be interesting to see how both cards will affect your year.

TAROT AS ORACLE

Y OU may be surprised that I'm not starting my book with this chapter. I want to talk about respect for the cards, and tarot (small "t" this time) as a tool.

What is tarot? Why does it work? Why *should* it work is a better question. There is nothing inherently magical (or magickal) about a deck of cards. They are paper, some colored inks, and maybe a thin plastic coating—nothing more. I can crack open a brand new deck from the bookstore and give you an accurate reading—no years of use or supernatural powers or occult rituals are necessary for working with these cards. Yet even so, the correct cards will pop up and will answer your question.

I am not a psychic, nor have I ever claimed to be one. I read the images in the cards from a purely scientific standpoint: I use the system laid out in this book, and it works for me. Many people including myself will tell you that the more you work with something, such as divination, the better you become at it. Can you develop your psychic skills? Of course you can. Will that help you with your readings? Yes, it will. Is it absolutely necessary? Well . . .

The images on Tarot cards are *archetypes*, defined as "the original . . . of which all things of the same type are copies" (*Webster's New Collegiate Dictionary*). Carl Jung, the psychologist who wrote so brilliantly about archetypes, was fascinated by Tarot; it fulfilled his concept that images and experiences are part of the unconscious and that we are *born* with them and recognize them instantly, even as infants. The image of the old crone, the prodigal son, the knight in shining armor, the lover, and the magician—we are born with them inside us. Many times when you are doing a reading and turn over a card, you will speculate on what it means, but the Querent will tell you immediately—"that's my father," "that's the fire at the garage," or "that's what happened last summer." The image on the card evokes a memory or triggers a thought process.

But why do those cards *turn up*? Why does someone who has never seen a Tarot card before shuffle and ask about something and have a card that relates to it come up? The law of averages?

There are many theories with both supporters and detractors.

The first "answer" is *synchronicity*—the concept that the universe is not the random playground it may seem to be, and that everything has *order*. Shuffling the cards is not a random act as much as it becomes an *ordering* act—consciously or unconsciously—whether with muscle spasms in the fingers or willful acts of the mind—the cards being shuffled are being put in that order. The people who "pooh-pooh" the idea that Tarot is mystical or occult favor this one.

A second theory deals with the human electromagnetic field, or the aura. Readers use the deck, and during that whole time it is within their aura. Studying the cards leaves an electric imprint on them ("this is a card about deceit"), so when a Querent shuffles and asks about possible deception, those cards are brought to the top and get read. I tend to favor this theory, but like I said, I can do a reading with a brand new deck of cards and still achieve a great deal of accuracy.

Another theory (usually supported by the religious fringe) is that evil spirits or demons control the cards. This group denies that such a world exists to begin with! But they still insist that we mere mortals are being deceived by evil into thinking we are divining or possibly that we are able to control our destinies.

Possibly somewhere between these three very different concepts lies the truth.

You will probably come up against those who say that you "are making it all up." To imply that I am "making it up" says that I am *lying*, that there is no basis for what I am doing. It says the images on the cards are meaningless, since I am telling you whatever I *feel* like telling you.

Others will say that "the cards don't tell you anything you don't already know." Sometimes Tarot does reflect back what Querents already know, but in an attempt to make them look at their situation, or to validate their feelings about something. Very often we refuse to look at what we know. When you get hit with these statements and attitudes—be direct if you have to. During one of my classes, a teacher appeared at the door to retrieve something from the storage closet. When he realized the subject I was teaching "in his room," he became very rude, questioning everything I was doing. I looked at him and replied, "I am not here for your entertainment, and I do not answer to you!" He quickly left. You can probably create some witty comebacks, but it's not worth your time or effort.

Another issue you'll be faced with is the "parlor game" mentality. People will tell you they had a grandmother or elderly aunt who "read cards." They will treat you as if you are playing a game with them, and wait to hear you tell them about "one-eyed Jacks" and other cartomancy stuff. These are the people who have seen one too many "dial 1-900-PSYCHIC" commercials and expect you to come to their house wearing cheap flashy turbans, caftans, and too much jewelry. They will want to know about "tall, dark strangers" met under lampposts on dark, stormy nights.

There is a certain entertainment value inherent in what we do, but I have found that these people are easily deflated when you start their reading and they find out that you are not only serious, but accurate. Most of these people will leave the table shaking their heads and wondering how you "got it right." (They also will probably seek you out for further readings.) I remember one medieval fair I went to—a friend came to see me while I was doing readings, and then went to visit another reader friend who was doing divination with Celtic trees. She was shocked that unbeknownst to either one of us, we gave her practically the same reading! She was expecting some kind of phony parlor magic and that she would be told what decision to make. We gave her something to think about.

The biggest problem may be dealing with disrespect—disrespect by others, but, even worse, by yourself. Oh, there's a time for silliness and a time for fun, but this behavior should not involve your cards. On an online Tarot forum I participate in, we once had an "argumentative discussion" about reading the cards in public restaurants. An Internet forum poster (someone who "posts" on electronic media) had gotten a bad attitude from a waitress when he pulled the cards out at the table, even though he claims he had done it before without any interference. He railed on and on about being in a public place, about the First Amendment, and so on. Now I, who have not only done readings but conducted classes in the coffee shop of the local Barnes & Noble bookstore, told him he was wrong. A restaurant, even a chain restaurant like the Denny's he was complaining about, is private property and the management can stop you from doing anything they don't like. Perhaps he should have taken the problem to the manager, but in all probability the manager would have had no choice but to support the employee, even if the waitress was being unreasonable.

Another poster complained about getting royally chewed out by a college professor for pulling out his cards and attempting to do a reading in the back of a classroom—*during class time!* There is a time and a place for everything. Whipping out that deck to show the world how cool you are is a bad move—it brings your cards down to the level of a children's toy. Being the "spiritual rebel" by leaving your cards on the coffee table where your born-again Christian in-laws are sure to see them is asking for trouble. Your ability to read the cards may diminish as a result.

Tarot is a tool; it is a means to an end, but is not the end in itself. Many people are frightened of Tarot cards, as though an unpleasant prediction will come true merely because the cards say so—as though the cards themselves have mystical powers to make something happen. Tarot will show you things that *can* happen, but it is no guarantee that they *will* happen. If the cards show that your job is destroying your health, will you stay in that job and have a heart attack? No, you will review your life and your resumé and try to find something better. That doesn't mean you still won't get sick down the road somewhere, but the minute you decide to change your job, you change the future predicted in that reading, no matter what it said.

Some people may disagree with me, but I say that Tarot is fallible—it is only as good as the person doing the reading. It is totally subjective—what readers see and how they put it together and how they ultimately predict an outcome depend on the capability of the reader. All the esoteric symbols in the world won't make a bit of difference if they are misinterpreted.

If you find yourself reading with a strange deck with different symbolism, what will you do? There are many "vanity" decks out there—theme decks that have lovely artwork but little substance, decks that sound like a great idea, but about halfway through, you realize the artist was getting tired or bored. But with experience (and time) you should be able to pick up just about any deck and do an acceptable reading with it.

As a tool Tarot has some limits. The problem for most beginners is that they bought or were given a deck, flipped through a book, got some degree of accuracy (sometimes), and then felt they were capable of doing and answering anything. Many people think that Tarot can (or will) answer any question, as though it is the "all-knowing, all-seeing infallible oracle" (bought for $19.95 and printed in Belgium). It is easy to see why. On the online forum, we once had to dissuade a young poster from expecting the "one, true, real, and completely honest answer to every question you have." She wanted to know if she should ask her cards if vampires are real. If you can't handle the answer—don't ask the question.

One issue that gets batted around quite often is the subject of payment—being paid to do a reading. Within "the craft" it has generally been considered improper to charge for magickal services. The idea is that, after all, your abilities are a gift and should be given freely. To receive payment (monetary or otherwise) would be acceptable, but to charge a set rate or fee is considered taboo. Robin Wood, artist and author of her own deck and book, does not charge a fee for readings because she feels that to do so creates a "contract" ("I'm paying you and I want a reading now!"), and sometimes she just doesn't feel like reading! By not charging a fee, she feels that she can set the time and place at her convenience, and is not pressured to "produce" at the whim of the Querent. (Obviously, the staff of the average "1-900" number does not share her sentiments—or wish to barter for their services.) I feel if you provide a service, you should receive compensation for that service. I have been criticized for this; in fact, I was heavily criticized for writing this book since the accuser felt that I "should freely teach" and writing this book was an affectation of greed. (His jealousy was apparent!)

A student once asked me about a message the cards gave him that he felt was unrelated to the question, or that didn't seem to answer the question at all. He was doing a reading for a woman whose mother was trying to sell her house. She wanted to know if the house would sell, and the cards gave her a reading about health issues. On the forum we discussed this for a while; most of us felt that for some reason the cards knew the mother's health issues were more important in the scheme of things than the selling of her house. The reader did not go into the card details, so we didn't pinpoint anything. But what causes a situation like this?

If the cards are controlled by the unconscious mind, perhaps the woman was thinking about her mother's health even though she was asking about the house sale. This happens quite frequently in readings. People think of many different things or get distracted, and the cards try to answer all the questions at the same time. This results in a muddled reading. This is why I object to reading in a public setting such as a restaurant. Distractions influence the cards. When I perform readings at a psychic fair, most times the readers have separate tables but they can be close to each other. This is not usually a problem, though. When I do a house party, the readings are conducted in another room away from the snacks and wine. This is also why I stopped working at the Mardi Gras, where the band, food, dancing, and readers were all in one room. First, having to shout over the band is not conducive to a good reading, and secondly, the carnival atmosphere is too intrusive. (Of course, people at a Mardi Gras are not going to ask you for the secret of the mystery of life—but why bring yourself down to such a low level?)

I had an interesting experience once where I was doing a reading through e-mail for a client. As I was working through the spread and starting to type it up, I realized that the spread had nothing to do with *his* relationship—but pertained to my own! I explained this and sent it to him with an explanation. Then I waited for a few days and did another reading for him. The second reading was more accurate. Why did the cards tell me about my relationship instead of his?

One reason, I believe, has to do with who shuffled the cards. My feeling (the aura theory, again) is that the person who does the shuffling adds his energies to the cards. There are readers who *never* let Querents touch the cards—all they are allowed to do is ask a question. I think it is better when the Querent makes a greater contribution to the energies of a reading. I have done readings over the phone, with the Querent telling me when to start and stop shuffling, and how to cut the pack. The phone line connects us. Although a Tarot reader is perfectly capable of doing a reading in absentia for someone (with his or her permission—never use the Tarot to "eavesdrop" on people's lives), I always feel a "live" reading is best. I explain to my e-mail clients that the cards will be slightly prejudiced, since they, the Querents, have no direct input into the reading.

The Next Step?

So, what then is your next step? I, myself, never expected to become a Tarot card reader when I began to use the cards; much less did I expect to be teaching classes, have a Tarot website, or write this book! It just happened and I took it for what it was worth. Eventually, I gave up reading the cards for myself, which I felt was the best idea in the long run, for I was too close to the subject to keep a true perspective. I searched until I found someone who could give me an unbiased, one-card daily reading. I dutifully record this in my journal. But no matter what your original intentions are when you start studying Tarot, someday, somewhere, someone is going to corner you and desperately ask you to do a reading . . . and you will.

I hope that you will seriously continue your study of Tarot, and that this book provides the springboard for you. I have found it to be a long and absolutely fascinating study. Tarot is a part of my daily life; I hold it in the highest regard. That is why throughout this book you have always found the word "Tarot" spelled with a capital "T." I wouldn't have rendered it any other way.

APPENDICES

Y OU will find few references to astrology in my book, even
  though there are many correlations between the two systems. I
feel astrology is a lifetime of study in its own right, and to layer
another system on top of this one would only confuse a beginner
with no basic understanding of either system.

Astrological Correspondences
   The Cups = Water signs: Cancer, Scorpio, Pisces
   The Wands = Fire signs: Aries, Leo, Sagittarius
   The Pentacles = Earth signs: Taurus, Virgo, Capricorn
   The Swords = Air signs: Gemini, Libra, Aquarius

You may find this helpful even if you are not ready to study
Tarot and astrology. Sometimes Querents will give you their birth
date and/or their astrological sign. When you turn over the King of
Pentacles and say that the person represented is an Earth sign,
many people who understand astrology are usually aware of which
signs they may or may not be compatible with. You are giving them
more information, and they in turn can validate what you have told
them. Likewise, when they have told you their intended is a Leo
and you turn over the Strength card, they suddenly will pay more
attention to the information you tell them.

Major Arcana Correspondences:
   Fool—Uranus, air
   Magician—Mercury
   High Priestess—Moon
   Empress—Venus
   Emperor—Aries, Spring Equinox

﹍﹍ant—Taurus, earth
﹍overs—Gemini, east
Chariot—Cancer
Strength—Leo
Hermit—Virgo
Wheel—Jupiter, west
Justice—Libra
Hanged Man—Neptune, water, Summer Solstice
Death—Scorpio
Temperance—Sagittarius
Devil—Capricorn, Autumnal Equinox
Tower—Mars, north
Star—Aquarius
Moon—Pisces
Sun—Sun, south, Winter Solstice
Judgment—Pluto, fire
World—Saturn

An Actual Reading

I did the following reading for a friend. On the surface, everything seemed like it was up front and simple to interpret, but it turned out not to be. This is how I present it as a homework assignment when I teach classes in card interpretation. I discuss the outcomes with the class and check and see what they come up with in response to my questions. I show them where I feel I was correct, and later where I feel I went so very wrong in this interpretation.

Do your own reading before examining my explanations or trying to second-guess the subtext.

The Celtic Cross Layout:
1) The Magician
2) Two of Cups
3) Page of Pentacles (clarified with the Five of Swords)
4) The Moon
5) Four of Pentacles
6) The Fool
7) Four of Wands
8) The Tower
9) Ten of Swords
10) Page of Wands (clarified with the Ace of Swords)

56-Year-Old Male

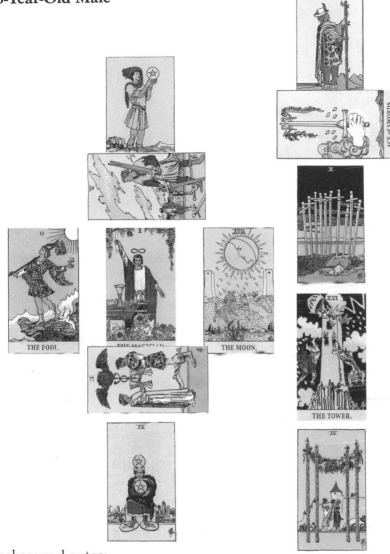

Background notes:

Frank is a 56-year-old schoolteacher at the top of his pay scale.

He has been married for almost 25 years, with no children.

He is out of work at the moment with an illness:

a) Is this illness long- or short-term in nature?

b) How would you interpret the last four cards (#7–#10)?

c) Does the situation resolve? Why or why not?

d) What is your conclusion?

e) If this reading was the product of your "one-on-one" with

nt, how would you have felt discussing cards such as The
e Ten of Swords with him?

Note: One essential piece of information is missing from the
background notes. When I assign homework, it is to judge how the
students' minds are working and to see whether I am getting
through—it is not to see whether they come up with the correct—
or my—answer. I look to see if the meanings of the cards that they
fill in and what they come up with as the reading have a connection. Sometimes students pull card meanings out of whatever
books they own, but then do not relate them to the reading they
are producing and do not create coherence.

One of the things that makes this reading more difficult for my
students is that there is no one there to talk with. If they were
sitting across from a real person, they would be able to ask questions or get responses that might help them clarify things in their
own minds. This is why I ask them how they would feel discussing
the Tower and Ten of Swords—cards that would get some kind of
emotional response from a real person.

Keeping all this in mind, here is the original interpretation from
my journal for Frank's cards:

Cards #1 to #3—the Core of the Question

An individual is trying to gain control over a situation with the
help of a loved one (Magician crossed by Two of Cups). When the
Page came up, I turned over a card to see what kind of news the
Page was bringing to this situation. I interpreted the Five of
Swords as telling me the situation will end in defeat.

Cards #4 to #6—the Past, Present, and Future

The Past has a history of defeats (illness); the Present is charac-
terized by trying to hold onto material things. The Future will be a
journey into the unknown.

Cards #7 and #8—the Internal and External

The individual is trying to maintain a stable front, although the
environment around him and his emotions become disastrous due
to dramatic changes or revelations.

Card #9—Hopes and Fears

He fears death, and dying.

Card #10—The Final Outcome
The Page brings important news; the Ace of Swords as its clarifier indicates victory after a long struggle.

All in all, this is a somewhat upbeat reading, even though the Querent fears that he will die, and the first conclusion card has the Five of Swords indicating defeat. The Second conclusion card is the Fool, who looks at the world around him with new eyes and is on a new journey. The final outcome says that he will be victorious, even though he fears he will die.

Most of my students decipher a major but short-term illness. Some predict surgery in his future, others see his marriage crumbling, and a few have seen him having an affair. Most students felt that they might be uncomfortable with the Tower and Ten of Swords cards, but felt that with a real person for the Querent they might be able to work through his fears. After all, the final outcome is definite—a victory—meaning he will recover. Doesn't he?

Ten days after I did this reading for Frank, he died at home, his health failing quickly. When I received the call that he was dead, I was stunned. Where had my interpretation gone wrong?

The one piece of information I leave out of the homework assignment is the fact that Frank was dying of cancer of the lymph nodes. All of his friends were well aware of it; we all knew he was dying. He had been through chemotherapy and other treatments, and we understood that he was going to die, but I felt that these cards did not predict his death. Hindsight being 20/20, I pulled out Frank's reading as soon as I hung up the phone. Tarot does not predict death; I have said this many times and I still firmly believe it does not. I sat there analyzing what I had already written with this new "final outcome" in mind and I came up with several reinterpretations.

I still accept the first three cards as described; the situation will end in defeat. Although Frank is trying to keep control over the situation and has the support of his wife, the situation will defeat them. After this point I reinterpret almost everything.

The Moon in the past is the breakdown of his health. His body deceives him, and in the Four of Pentacles (the Miser) he struggles to hold onto his health. The future becomes the amazement of the Fool as a new journey begins. *What* journey? How did we get from the struggles of the Five of Swords to the childlike Fool off to explore the wonders of the universe?

ly, he hopes to maintain a quiet front, to show that
still under control, but those around him are aware
defeat of the illness by medical treatments is acknowl-
edged as only temporary. His fears of death are not unfounded.

However, we still come to that Final Outcome of "victory over strife." How does Frank go from defeat to a new beginning to victory over his pain and suffering? His illness is terminal! My new conclusion was that there is only one way he would find that peace—and that is by dying. I still believe that the cards did what they do best: they gave me a gentle conclusion to accept, and they themselves do not predict his death. "Seeing" death in the cards is not the same as the cards "predicting" his death; the revelation and responsibility fall back on the reader. My students are usually devastated at this conclusion.

What do you think? Did the cards predict his death, and did I miss it, or am I overreacting in hindsight?

ACKNOWLEDGMENTS

I would like to acknowledge the following authors, whose works have been constant inspirations to me, both in how I developed my classroom lectures and in their abilities to create simple answers to my students' complicated questions. I am eternally indebted to them.

Nancy Garen: *Tarot Made Easy*, 1989. For teaching me how to put the "spin" on a Tarot card to make it fit a given situation.

Eden Gray: *Mastering the Tarot*, 1971, and *The Tarot Revealed*, 1988, two books that will stand the test of time.

Richard T. Kaser: *Tarot in Ten Minutes*, 1992. For his "all questions are only four questions" concept and the definitions of the card themes.

Arlene Tognetti & Lisa Lenard: *The Complete Idiot's Guide® to Tarot and Fortune Telling*, 1999. For their understanding of the Court cards.

INDEX